ADVENTURING IN PRIESTHOOD

Walter Forde

Adventuring in Priesthood

THE COLUMBA PRESS
DUBLIN 1993

First edition, 1993, published by
THE COLUMBA PRESS
93 The Rise, Mount Merrion, Blackrock, Co Dublin

ISBN 1 85607 082 4

Cover by Bill Bolger
Origination by The Columba Press
Printed by Loader Jackson Printers, Arlesey

Copyright © 1993, Walter Forde

Contents

Acknowledgements 6
Preface *by Bishop Brendan Comiskey* 7
Introduction: My Story 11

PART I: PRIEST, PARISH AND CHURCH

Chapter 1: The Priestly Task 18
Chapter 2: Seminary Training 24
Chapter 3: Celibacy 27
Chapter 4: A National Pastoral Plan 30
Chapter 5: The Parish Today 33
Chapter 6: The Parish and Pastoral Planning 42
Chapter 7: 'Pay, Pray and Obey' 52

PART II: THE CHURCH AND SOCIETY

Chapter 8: Beware the Emperor's Embrace 64
Chapter 9: No Sacristy Priest 71
Chapter 10: Groups with Special Needs 86
Chapter 11: The New Creation and the New Generation 102
Chapter 12: Working with Young People 110
Chapter 13: Communicate or Die 119
Chapter 14: The Religious Press in Ireland 130
Chapter 15: Counter Witness 138

Acknowledgements

There are many people to whom I am indebted. My family, Maura, Ken, Clionadh, Aoife and Kenneth, for their support in so many ways over the years and 'the countless unremembered acts of kindness and of love'.

Bishop Brendan Comiskey for his unfailing encouragement, support and kindness; all those with whom I have worked, either in organisations or in the parish, for their insights and dedication, especially those with whom I now work, Canon John Gahan, Frs Matt Kelly and Jimmy Moynihan, Canon Philip Knowles and Rev Roy Cooper; Liz Kavanagh who typed this book, for her cheerful patience; Peggy O'Gorman who has looked after me so well in Gorey for nineteen years; John Woodbyrne for his continuing help in so many aspects of parish life; Revv Tony O'Connell, Jimmy Moynihan, John Carroll and Jim Fitzpatrick for reading the proofs and providing some helpful suggestions; all my other close friends whose friendship and support has meant more than they will ever realise.

I am also indebted to Rev Ronan Drury, editor of *The Furrow*, and Rev Bernard Treacy OP, editor of *Doctrine and Life*, for allowing me to use material which originally appeared in their journals.

To all of you I am deeply grateful.

Preface

✠ Brendan Comiskey
BISHOP OF FERNS

The author of this book recently celebrated the 25th anniversary of his ordination to the priesthood. On the 'big night' itself, someone remarked that he 'closed down the town'.

It was more than the usual outpouring of praise which took place on the night. It was truly a 'community celebration'. It was taken so seriously by the community that a good and otherwise gentle lady remarked to me on the way out, 'If you move Father Forde from this town, I'll have you kneecapped!'

The author of this book writes out of the rich experience of his life and work, and the attitude he brings to his record of the past twenty-five years is one of realism and gratitude. The title of this book is evocative of optimism and hope: *Adventuring in Priesthood*. There has been too little information on the priesthood and ministry coming 'from the trenches' as it were, and how can theologians theologise about a subject unless they are in possession of dispatches from the front? Father Walter Forde supplies them with a great deal of the most practical matter to be worked over.

His optimism is one without illusion and he does not shrink from listing and expanding on what we are doing wrong or failing to do at all. In addition to pursuing topics of on-going and urgent concern in the life of the Church, for example, the matter of full and active participation in the life of that Church, ecumenism, the Church and the media, he is honest and forthright in handling subjects such as celibacy without fear or favour.

This priest's life has been marked in a particular way by his involvement with youth and youth movements at local, diocesan and national level, and those who would wish to learn more about what Church and State have done in this area will find much that is interesting here.

However, it is in the area of the Church's involvement with the media, that he has become singularly engaged in more recent times, especially through his work with the Religious Press Association, local Southeast Radio and the cooperation of all the Churches through the Christian Media Trust in this venture. In addition, he is the Editor of the *Ferns Diocesan Bulletin* and Press Officer for the diocese.

He is a man of his age and the one great defining moment of his age and of his priestly ministry has been the Second Vatican Council. This book, in the simplest and most direct of ways, goes straight to the heart of what that Council was about: the mystery of the Church and the Church's role vis à vis the world, or, more simply put, the Church: what she is and what she does. His total conviction that the Church either communicates or dies comes from no desire to be a publicity seeker but from an understanding that the Church *is* in fact a communication: the Word made flesh.

In this priest's life there is a great respect not only for the role of journalists in society but also an appreciation and, indeed, an affection for most practitioners of that profession. His relations with the media are civil, courteous and warm.

But one communicates, of course, with one's whole life and not merely in writing or occasional appearances on radio or television and the priest-in-parish must do this in the home, in the school, in the hall, in sick-rooms and hospitals, in times of sadness as well as of celebration. Father Forde quotes with obvious approval a piece from an Australian journal:

> It is easy to make speeches and claims, but claims must be validated by the product. You are the means by which the good life advocated by the Church is communicated to people.

This is the other great challenge of the Vatican Council II: engagement with the world, a world God loved so much that he gave his only son to save it. The various headings in this book are records of those engagements, especially with the emigrants and the handicapped, the unemployed and the carers in the community who are too often overlooked. Ecumenism, seminary formation, pastoral planning; these are among his many concerns. And, of course, running through it all is his determination that the ministry of the Lord will never succeed in diverting his attention from the Lord of the ministry.

John Gardner once said that the last things that American society needed were the unloving critic and the uncritical lover. When it comes to writing about his twenty-five years of service, Father Forde is neither of these.

May *Adventuring in Priesthood* not only encourage all critical lovers of the Church, but may it also give many other priests engaged in ministry the courage and the confidence to set down on paper the triumphs and tragedies, the joys and sorrows, the adventures and adversities, through, with and in which they pilgrimage their way homewards.

Introduction: My Story

I have been ordained just over twenty five years. It is a good life, difficult at times, lonely at times, pressurised at times, but equally fulfilling, challenging and exciting. On balance I would honestly have to say that I would take the same path if I was eighteen again.

I grew up in Bunclody, on the Wexford/Carlow border and at the foot of Mount Leinster, which was a very pleasant, relaxed, rural community and parish – a town with a population, then, of less than a thousand.

My father was principal of the Primary School. In the tradition of school masters of that day, he was a key figure in the community and in the Church and had a great sense of commitment to both, putting in hours and days way above the call of duty.

My mother, who had a deep interest in people and a strong sense of duty, came from rural Clare. In summer my sister and I enjoyed the visits to Rynomona, a small townland in Clare, made famous by Arnsberg in his book the 'Irish Country Man'. He wrote in great detail about some of the local figures, including my grandfather who had the title 'The Public Prosecutor'. At any rate, out in the Clare Burren in an old rambling thatched house, without electricity or water, I had probably the most memorable and enjoyable summers of my life. I remember being struck by the tremendous sense of community and inter-dependence of neighbours, with gatherings every night, playing cards, telling ghost stories, exchanging gossip and occasionally singing and dancing. Neither of my grandparents had been further from home than Limerick. The local paper and the Sunday papers were the only newspapers people saw. On Sunday afternoon they usually listened to a match on an unwieldly wireless. It was light years away from the mobility and the communications and the gadgets of our age, but they were truly happy holidays.

Bunclody, when I was growing up in the fifties, was marked by a simple life. Religion and the priest were very central. It was a happy time. I can remember that our pleasures and pastimes were simple – marbles in the Spring, conkers in the Autumn, games of rounders and fishing and building cabins in the woods during the Summer.

The key in our front door was left there, often overnight. People were in and out of each other's houses. The street in which I grew up also was unusual in Ireland, in that it was 50% Church of Ireland and 50% Roman Catholic. We related to each other and we played together in the most natural of ways. I was amazed, in 1967 in Maynooth, when our class did a link up with the Anglican Divinity Students Hostel in Rathgar, and one of my classmates was meeting, or even seeing, a Protestant for the first time.

All in all, I think my childhood was happy and secure. Going to boarding school was a very strange and traumatic experience for me and I still have serious queries about the wisdom of large boarding schools. In my experience they can excessively toughen young people, suppress normal feelings, and in some cases stunt the development to maturity. At a later stage, in a Youth Club, we found that young people who were away at boarding school were less spontaneous, less natural, and less willing to get involved than those who had not had the boarding school experience.

The most difficult question to answer is: why did I become a priest? I would single out three broad factors in the decision. Firstly: I was attracted to the priesthood as a job, as other people are attracted to teaching, carpentry, medicine and so on. I felt that I would be happy and fulfilled at that. Secondly: My family was friendly with several priests who were regular callers to our home. My parents also had both respect and affection for the priesthood and a very strong commitment to the Church. Thirdly: The priesthood as lived by the priests I knew, and in particular by two, impressed me. One was a parish priest, very ordinary and not a little eccentric, but very caring of people and especially the sick and wounded ones of this world. Then there was priest teaching in St Peter's College in Wexford, where I studied, who was warm and kind, happy and outgoing. It was reasons such as these that prompted me to have a shot at it by going to Maynooth to learn more about the priesthood and about myself.

Maynooth, when I went there, boasted that the daily routine and the approach to formation was the same basically as they were in 1795. Then, in the middle of my time in Maynooth, the effects of Vatican II began to strike very quickly. It was indeed an enriching, liberating and idealistic experience. I think something of that combination of the strong discipline and the positive vision certainly stood to me since then.

To work as a priest
There are basically four types of situation that a diocesan priest can work in: As a priest in a parish (and in Ferns Diocese there are one hundred and four parishes and half-parishes); as a fulltime teacher (and we have a number of these in St Peter's College and in some Vocational Schools); as a missionary priest outside Ireland (and our Diocese has had a Diocesan Mission to Brazil for twelve years); in a fulltime administrative or specialist job, for example, as Director of Youth Services, Director of Family Life Services, head of a school, or in fulltime Diocesan administration.

I was lucky to have experience of three of these four types of appointment. For four years after ordination I was teaching Greek and Latin in St Peter's College, not indeed with any great success. I still teach Social Science one day a week at St Peter's Seminary, Wexford. For almost two years I was General Secretary of the

National Federation of Youth Clubs, which was then at an important development stage and that experience was a very stretching and exciting one for me. For the past nineteen years I have been curate in Gorey, which has been the most satisfying of all my appointments.

After my experiences working with the National Federation of Youth Clubs and having direct experience and involvement with priests and youth projects in most dioceses in the country, I looked at the diocese of Ferns and its traditions in a new light. It is an extremely pleasant diocese to work in. It is compact and we are probably unique in Ireland in that, apart from the five main towns, curates live on their own in the half-parishes, with church, school and community centres being their direct responsibility. In many ways they are parish priests of their half-parish. This leads to a degree of freedom and flexibility that is creative and generates a high level of morale. That, no doubt, is a factor in the high number of vocations to the priesthood. We have a surplus of over twenty priests who are on loan to other dioceses or doing special training. We are fortunate in that the last three bishops have been from outside the diocese: James Staunton, (Ossory, 1939-1963), Donald Herlihy, (Kerry, 1964-1983), Brendan Comiskey, SSCC, our present bishop.

We have always taken pride in the fact that relations between the bishop and the clergy have been particularly warm and Bishop Comiskey has often commented on the spontaneous welcome he received on his appointment and on his pastoral visitation of parishes in the diocese. There is, furthermore, a long tradition of friendship and co-operation with Christians of other Churches, of whom about five thousand live in this diocese. This is most clearly highlighted in recent times by the establishment by the two bishops of a joint inter-church committee which, for example, has produced several reports on inter-church marriages and so on.

Twenty-five years on
Looking back over twenty-five years, I am struck by the unexpect-

ed and unpredictable way things have developed, the interests and involvements, and the activities covered in the following chapters. I certainly would not have predicted them in 1968 when my expectation was that I would be likely to be teaching for twenty five years. That's where the 'Adventure' concept in the title comes from.

When I was ordained first, I was regularly annoyed when other priests contrasted their realism with my idealism and the clear implication was that they would like to help rid me of this dangerous idealism. I hope I have retained some of this idealism, the willingness to try new things, and the conviction that things can be better. All that is part of the adventure too.

* * *

These chapters are basically positive because I do feel positive about the Church at the grassroots in Ireland. Of course there have been problems and weaknesses. I believe very deeply that, like all Christians, priests are not born but made. We are always becoming Christian and becoming a priest. We are always, up to the end of our lives, growing, developing, trying, failing and starting again. We are each of us 'wounded healers', seeking healing ourselves and at the same time trying to bring it to others and to our world. Perhaps some of the failures have not been sufficiently highlighted in what follows, but then there is no scarcity of commentators prepared to do that for the Church.

* * *

To finish this introduction, I want to include a favourite piece of mine from Karl Rahner:

> My brothers, accept us as we are: The priest is not an angel sent from heaven. He is a man chosen from among men, a member of the Church, a Christian.
>
> Remaining man and Christian, he begins to speak to you the word of God. This word is not his own. No, he comes to you because God has told him to proclaim God's word. Perhaps

he has not entirely understood it himself. Perhaps he adulterates it. But he believes, and despite his fears he knows that he must communicate God's word to you.

For must not some one of us say something about God, about eternal life, about the majesty of grace in our sanctified being; must not some one speak of sin, the judgement and mercy of God?

So my dear friends, pray for us, carry us so that we may be able to sustain others by bringing to them the mystery of Gods' love revealed in Christ Jesus.

PART I

Priest, Parish and Church

CHAPTER 1

The Priestly Task

Two years ago I was doing a half day session on Priesthood for a group of school leavers at a Vocations Workshop. They were all seventeen or eighteen years old, which meant that I was ordained for five or six years before any of them were born. So we were coming from very different experiences, backgrounds and starting points.

To try to bridge the gap I did an exercise with them. I asked them to imagine going to live and to work in Saudi Arabia where there are no Christian Churches and no priests. They become friendly with a native family there who ask them to describe in simple, clear terms what a priest is. I asked these young people individually to take ten minutes to write a pen picture of a priest. We then jotted down the main points on a flip chart and elaborated on them.

This is what emerged. It shows the many sided and varied nature of the priest's life and work. Every priest knows that this can cause huge pressure and stress, yet most parishioners don't fully appreciate the hours involved or the pressures and the demands of the job.

The Role of the Priest
Reconciler: of divisions and conflict in life; a bringer of peace, understanding, sensitivity, care and concern. A reconciler between God and the individual (in the Sacrament of Reconciliation), in society; in family, in group.

Consoler: The gospel of Jesus Christ is about hope, love, healing

and consolation. 'I have carved you in the palm of my hands', 'If a mother forgot her child, I will not forget you.' This message a priest brings also in specific situations, such as death, tragedies, accidents. Whenever there is a sense of failure, separation etc., there he tries to bring hope and help.

Leader: He has a central role as a full-time trained leader of the Christian Community and, to some degree, of the wider local community. A leader is one who has vision, has courage to state his views and defend them, and who has commitment and dedication. Sometimes too there is an important leadership role that he can exercise in situations such as housing, unemployment, wealth distribution, social issues, etc.

Prophet: A person who has a vision of how things could be – how to build a better world, how to improve things. A person of sensitivity and with a Christian and critical eye.

Prayer: Listening and talking to God, becoming conscious of God's presence and action amongst us. God talks in terms of what we know. We find him 'in bits and pieces' of ordinary life (Kavanagh). So silence and quietness and setting aside some time and space each day for prayer is important.

Preacher/Teacher: He explains, and tries to understand more fully and help others to understand, the Christian Message in all its fullness. For that reason a trainee priest spends six or seven years studying the message and how to communicate it. He tries to see the mysteries of life.

Liturgist: He has a key role in the Sacraments: Baptism, Eucharist, Marriage, Confession, The Sacrament of the Sick and in various prayer services.

A Companion on the Journey: We all are pilgrims on a journey that begins with baptism and ends in eternity. We believe too that Jesus has made the journey before, returns to be with us as we travel, and is there at the end of the journey to welcome us. The priest travels the same journey himself and he is a companion to his people and needs their support and encouragement.

Because religion and priesthood touch every aspect of human life, and the deepest parts of the human experience, there is an unpredictability, an openness and a 'living on the knife edge' quality about it, of necessity. I have not gone into the debate about the future of ministry or the efforts to redefine priesthood in any detail. Much of the debate, in my view, is unreal, inadequately developed and unrelated to the real experience or the context in which priesthood is lived.

Priesthood can never be prepackaged nor can definitions eliminate the inevitable relational and other conflicts and uncertainties. Any priest who respects the many faceted nature of priesthood and tries to live it out honestly and conscientiously in the concrete circumstances of his own life has defined priesthood and given it 'a local habitation and a name.' I hope, in this book, my own concrete understanding and 'definition' of the priesthood emerges.

This is the ideal. What is the reality of the work?

About ten years ago I decided to log my activities in a given month, in fact to do a 'time and motion' study of myself. Ronan Drury gave it the very apt title in *The Furrow*, 'The Hours I Keep'.

Here is a Summary:

> Liturgy and Prayer (25.09%)
> Masses, Baptism, Confessions, Blessing of the Sick, Funerals, Marriages and Inter-Church Services, A Home Mass for a Golden Jubilee.
>
> Education (6.9%)
> Work in school with pupils and students. School based programmes and parish adult education sessions.
>
> Pastoral Care (29.43%)
> Visiting people in their homes; counselling people who call to me; visiting the sick in hospitals and nursing homes or in connection with some serious occasion in their lives.
>
> Social and Community Activities (15.63%)
> Meetings, projects and activities of the local Social Services

Council, Community Development Group and Association for the Handicapped.

Administration (11.27%)
Church meetings, routine correspondence, documentation about weddings etc. School and Parish fundraising, meetings and functions.

Responsibilities outside the Parish (11.8%)
Teaching two classes a week in the seminary. Press Officer for the Diocese and some committee work with the Irish Commission for the Laity and the Irish Youth Foundation.

My view at the time was: 'This whole analysis has been helpful to me. Just putting things on paper and studying them brings out a number of lessons, some of which I have taken on board. I was genuinely surprised by the proportionate breakdown. The disparity would be greater if one compared the above with a theoretical description of what the priesthood was about. This highlights, for example, the extent to which local pressures and expectations have a strong influence on how the priest spends his time. It also underlines the wide range and variety of demands on his time, while very few people realise the time put in on the job, or the sheer pressure of conflicting demands. Equally, this means that there is little time for reflection, for analysis, for consultation and for long-term planning.'

Planning, methodology and self management are of crucial importance for the priest. There is an accepted distinction in management between active and re-active tasks. The active and positive tasks are the ones you must do to initiate change and achieve development. The re-active tasks are all the day to day events and demands of the job. There was little enough of the active tasks in my rota when I examined it in detail. There are now many specialised individuals and agencies in each diocese whom the priest can call on for advice, information, ideas and practical help. In my work for that month there was no concrete way in which I availed of these or linked my work with the broader issues and concerns of the Church outside my parish.

I feel that there are some wider implications for the Church in this, both in terms of pastoral formation and pastoral planning. Before going on to reflect on those topics, I would like to end this chapter with three of my favourite quotations about the priesthood:

In *Parish Leadership Today*, George Martin says:

> How did Jesus establish his Church? Not by waiting for people to seek him out. He went into the streets and along the waterfront recruiting. He chose men for service and asked them to follow him. He chose some very unlikely people. Fishermen are not generally at the forefront of religious revolutions. But he saw in these men he chose the potential for them to become the foundation of his Church. He walked up to them when they were busy and asked them to set those things aside and to follow him and they did this.

Edward Farrell says:

> The priest is a man on a journey.
> He is a pilgrim of the absolute.
> He is a God-hunting and a God-hunted man.
>
> He has been touched by the finger of God
> because he is a man called.
>
> He is continually meeting people at the deep
> part of their lives, at the depths of their
> anguish and sin, prayer and love.
>
> He is continually being hollowed out.
> Each day he goes to the mountain, the altar,
> is the great receiver of the Gift which
> he is to minister to his brothers and sisters.

> The word of God cuts into him a little
> more deeply each time.
> His people scar him and give him their
> wounds for healing.

> The priesthood never ceases to be a
> radical religious experience.

St Paul says:

> I have been made a servant of the Church by God, who gave me this task to perform for your good. It is the task of fully proclaiming his message, which is the secret he hid through all past ages from all mankind, but has now revealed to his people. God's plan is this: To make known his secret to his people, this rich and glorious secret which he has for all peoples. And the secret is this: Christ is in you, which means that you will share the glory of God.

CHAPTER 2

Seminary Training

It is truly traumatic to shift from the safe, close, secure world of a small seminary, to becoming a leader in the Christian community. Depending on age, background, education, people's expectations of the priest and the Church are different. The priest has to try to respond to differing and sometimes conflicting expectations. Unlike any other profession, the priest has to work on a daily basis with a whole cross-section of people whose attitudes, perspectives and responses are different from each other's. Unlike any other professions too, people's decision to participate in the Church or approach the priest is a totally 'voluntary' one.

I have great admiration for how well the younger priest copes with this. The culture shock involved in being appointed to a parish on their own is intense. There is no doubt in my mind that some loose support structures for priests are extremely important. We all need mentors at every stage of our priesthood. We need some close friends, lay and clerical, who can support us and affirm us. We also need some non-threatening and relaxed informal groupings for priests on occasions where people can unwind and talk through their difficulties. I find that younger priests are in some ways more self-contained than we were. They are rightly much more conscious of their own developmental needs and their rights than we were, and they also have a better facility to relate naturally to people. They are very close and supportive to priests of their own age group and are very effective preachers.

Having said all that, life as a priest for them is much more pressurised than it was in our day and it makes it all the more important that structures, procedures and programmes be in place. This leads to the question of seminary formation. Having had the experience of being trained as a social worker, and comparing it with my training for the priesthood, I have to say that the seminary training was seriously inadequate.

In my view the greatest single weakness of the seminary training is its lack of concrete pastoral orientation and systematic pastoral training. The emphasis still seems to be on theoretical training, rather than on pastoral training, which helps them to 'use' themselves as individuals rather than work as members of a team. The training in preaching and catechetics has greatly improved but seminarians do not get an overall pastoral approach. Does their training help them to see where overall priorities are? How difficulties as a whole can be tackled? How their work fits in with the Church's overall priorities and plan? Does it expose them to the wide range of experiences and situations they may be faced with? The range of functions they will have to fulfil? The needs they will have to meet? Above all, does it give them skills to be able to cope with these and to plan their own lives and the programme of their parish? To what extent does the seminary formation include training in working with groups, counselling, skills of listening and perceiving, how to organise and administer, techniques of motivating people, and over-view of parish life and functions? I suspect the answer to any of these questions is either no or not fully.

The priesthood is probably the only one of the 'caring' professions for which there is no supervised apprenticeship or in-depth training in job skills or relational skills. Seminarians do have programmes of visits to agencies, organisations or situations but these are of very limited value unless they have been carefully prepared, are monitored during the visits and are assessed later.

This supervision and direction can only effectively be given by someone who has both pastoral experience and some specialised training himself. In most dioceses now there are at least a few priests with training in the pastoral care of specialised groupings – the young, those in hospital, school students, the elderly, the disabled, families, and so on. They, in conjunction with the parish clergy, liturgists, catechists, administrators, social workers and seminary staff, could help devise a worthwhile programme of pastoral training and could also be involved as supervisors and tutors during the courses.

I feel that pastoral placements right through the four years theology programme would be worthwhile. These should be supportive and challenging and would provide seminarians with the experience of the reality of priesthood and pastoral life before they actually made a diaconate decision. Placement is also important for another reason. Going to a seminary is not simply going to a new and more advanced college with a new uniform, new subjects or a different programme. First and foremost, it is offering oneself for service in a particular diocese. No longer an individual, the student should become part of the mission of this diocese in a specialised way and should be taken into the life and work of the diocese gradually and according to his capabilities.

It is also desirable that every seminarian would have had an opportunity, for six months or a year, of working at a normal job away from home, either before or during the seminary course.

The first two years of the seminary programme should include strong elements of personal development, social development and faith development programmes.

The entry age to the seminary is something that should be looked at. Seventeen or eighteen is too young an age to accept seminarians. Equally, a person should not be ordained to the priesthood before the age of twenty-five. Those who have to spend an extra year as seminarians because of their very young age should use that year on some specialised programme linked to their own personal needs and talents.

This topic of pastoral training remains a crucial area for thought and development, one of the unfulfilled tasks of renewal in the Irish Church.

CHAPTER 3

Celibacy

In the aftermath of the Bishop Casey affair, I was truly amazed by the number of middle-of-the-road, even conservative Catholics who quite spontaneously said to me they thought that priests should be allowed to get married. There is no doubt in my mind that for many devout Catholic lay people compulsory celibacy is in no way a forceful witness to higher values. Freely chosen, celibacy can be a striking witness to other worldly values and it can, if freely undertaken, unleash a great outpouring of love, generosity, self-sacrifice and service.

Celibacy has an important and long established place in the Christian Church. St Paul mentioned the practical advantages of remaining unmarried to do the Lord's Work. Jesus himself is presumed to have been celibate and had proposed it as a free act of obedience to a special vocation and as a spiritual gift for the sake of the Kingdom.

Donna Tiernan Mahoney's book, *Touching the Face of God*, has this to say:

> Until optional celibacy is accepted by the Church, it will be impossible for the Church to be the proclaimer of justice that she is called to be. Celibacy will only be accepted as valuable and powerful if it is chosen.

To offer a different perspective, I asked a friend of mine who is a deacon and preparing for the priesthood how he viewed his celibacy. This was his response: 'Two roads diverged in a yellow wood, and I took the one less travelled by, and that has made all the difference.'

ADVENTURING IN PRIESTHOOD

Those are the words of Robert Frost and I feel that they are appropriate to this subject, in that the road of priesthood and of celibacy are indeed less travelled. I think it's also true that there are many more diversions and by-roads off this road than ever. The subject of priestly celibacy is one that comes up at every juncture. It evokes one of two responses, either a calm logical account of what celibacy is, or a heated and angry monologue about how bad it is.

However we deal with the issue, we must admit that it is something we all have a definite opinion on. Personally I look at it from a positive point of view which in many ways may be rare.

To start at the beginning, Christ hung, bled and died on a cross for me. For me as an individual, so that I may have life and have it to the full. The only reasonable response I can have to this is to offer my life back in its entirety, warts and all as it were. My response can be nothing less than everything. Having come to see it in that way, I come to see celibacy as a part of my giving back to God. If I don't, then I'm not giving him all I can. It's like the story of God coming to look at a house belonging to a man. The house is really the man himself. The man says, 'I'll rent you two rooms.' 'I don't want to rent, I want to buy,' says God. 'Well I'm not sure,' says the man 'Maybe later I can give you more'. 'I can wait,' says God, 'I like what I see.' God will wait for our response but we have to let him buy the house that is ourselves and let his Son come live in it in order to obtain the room we need for ourselves.

Unfortunately, mandatory celibacy has created serious problems. Excellent men are leaving to get married. There is no doubt that it is preventing many fine young people from making the choice of priesthood and it has created personal difficulties for many other priests. Increasingly, it is the view of large number of people that celibacy is an abnormal situation. There is clear enough evidence, I think, that the vocation shortage is long-term. The social pressures causing the downturn in vocations are proactive and, under present discipline, the Church is powerless to reverse. Officially few priests are leaving the ministry. The reality is quite different. I read somewhere, (and unfortunately I am unable to locate the quotation), about a year ago, an article which suggested that the vocation shortage was so severe that at the moment the equivalent of half the Catholic parishes in the world are without a priest or an adequate number of priests. If celibacy were made optional, we probably would have a surplus of priests by the early part of the next century.

For the first ten centuries the Church never thought of making celibacy a condition for ordination. Peter was married. So, probably, were all the other apostles except John. So were many of the early Popes and lower clergy. It was Pope Gregory VII who made celibacy mandatory. He offered it as a sign of dedication to the priesthood, but in part he was concerned with church property being willed to families of priests.

Expanding the permanent diaconate and developing more lay ministries have eased the vocations crisis. Both these solutions have limits. As long as the institutional issues of power and control are linked to male celibate life, such options would have limited effectiveness.

The Eucharist is at the heart of the Christian community. To have the Eucharist in every Christian community is more important than a law of the Church about celibacy.

There has been a reluctance to openly and honestly discuss the problems created by celibacy. I would dearly like to see a survey on a professional and confidential basis conducted by an agency like the National Conference of Priests about the real experiences of celibacy as opposed to the theory of celibacy which makes the running at the moment.

CHAPTER 4

A National Pastoral Plan

One of the important needs in the Irish Church, and one for which the National Conference of Priests has called again and again, is a National Pastoral Plan, to which Pope John Paul II referred in 1992 during the ad limina visit of the Irish Episcopal Conference. This would be an overall statement of pastoral direction – What particular pastoral problems are important just now? How should they be responded to and how should personnel and resources be marshalled in the most effective and professional way? What are the priorities for action? How are they related to each other? What time-scales will be followed? and so on.

As part of their recommendations for the special meeting of the Irish Episcopal Conference, held at Killeshandra to decide the follow-up to the Pope's visit, the NCPI recommended the National Pastoral Plan. There was a clear consensus among the members of the NCPI as to the sort of plan needed – 'not another document handed down from the bishops or someone else, distributed among the priests and then shelved.' It asked that all sections of the Church should be involved in working out and in implementing this plan.

The bishops decided not to promote a National Pastoral Plan at that time but, instead, to commend pilot schemes at diocesan and parish levels. The bishops did not indicate what kind of pilot schemes they had in mind, or how they were to be initiated or monitored. Over thirteen years later, it is not clear if any such official pilot schemes were ever launched at parish or diocesan level, or whether they were successes or failures.

The need for a comprehensive, well-researched and imaginative National Pastoral Plan is even more crucial today.

Planning Procedure

Planning procedure involves a number of clear stages in any organisation.

(1) *Research.* Every organisation has specific goals which it tries to achieve in the most effective possible way. Research is always important in assessing its effectiveness in achieving these objectives, in discovering the exact nature and dimensions of failures and needs, and in building up an accurate picture of the social background and conditions in which it works. Linked to this would be discussion and experimentation at all levels of the Church, the results of which are monitored, assessed and communicated to those in decision-making position.

(2) *Policy Decisions.* The highest management level in any organisation makes some basic policy decisions as to how the goals of the organisation can be achieved. In the case of the Church this means deciding what particular pastoral objectives should be treated as priorities?

(3) *Planning.* An ideal is proposed in general terms as an objective that the Church wishes to see implemented as a priority. Concrete suggestions need to be made with each proposal as to how it can be implemented. The National Church Commissions could be involved in devising a plan and in developing guidelines and directions for implementation of the plan. What would emerge then is the outline of a National Plan which would be backed up by pastoral plans at diocesan, deanery and parish levels.

(4) *Execution.* Clergy need to feel that if a proposal is made, they all have a responsibility to see that it is implemented and that in fact there is some supervisory mechanism which will check whether, and to what extent, it has been implemented. Clergy conferences could be built around such pastoral planning and they would have a key role in implementing such decisions.

The individual priest needs to have fairly immediate and regular access to skilled personnel who will help him to implement the plan in his own area. The specialist people listed in the Irish Catholic Directory (for each diocese) might have responsibility for a pastoral proposal which falls within their competence.

(5) *Re-Assessment.* Some system of re-assessing the approach, of examining different strategies and of redefining methods needs to be devised. In general terms, the structures and procedures in the Church do not operate very effectively or smoothly along these lines. These tasks do not take place separately or in as smooth a sequence as they should. Some bits happen too loosely and are unconnected with one another. There are, for example, too few levels of management in the Church and therefore too many tasks are predominantly or exclusively concentrated among too few people.

There are still too few specialised personnel, or at least too few with real influence in the local Church.

CHAPTER 5

The Parish Today

One of the most fundamental and central facts of Irish Catholic life is the parish system. Its role commands attention and its changing nature demands study. The Irish parish is a venerable institution. Even today it is possible to trace many parish boundaries back to the middle ages with virtually no adjustment.

The parish system has served well in the past. Will it continue to serve as well in the future? In what ways does it need to be adapted and supplemented to meet the changes of the new social setting and theological understanding? What are its most important functions? Are we impressed by features of the parish system – its extent, its building, its range of activities – but unaware that its Christian character and impact don't remain a force to the extent they were in the past? Are there not major new Christian developments taking place which have little or no relationship with the parish system? Has the parish become a sort of religious sideshow with little enough bearing on life or real relevance to people?

These are some of the questions that would suggest themselves to parochial clergy reflecting their unease about the effectiveness of the parish today.

Despite this questioning and this unease, there is very little detailed writing, research and discussion on the parish. There is no monitoring of individual initiatives or writing up of particular projects, no real sharing of approaches and experience of the parish system. There is a real need for systematic development of the parish system. That means more research, serious discussion and worthwhile writing on the parish, its strengths and weaknesses, its relationship with other parishes and with the diverse community in which it operates.

The parish is the grouping through which people primarily and permanently identify with the Church. Increasingly, too, it is recognised that pastoral services and programmes succeed only if they are parish based.

Weaknesses of the contemporary parish

The parish system suited well the static homogeneous society of the past, with fixed boundaries and stable populations. But a single, all-purpose model of the parish is clearly inadequate today. The social settings, the problems, the needs and the possibilities vary greatly from one type of parish to another. The traditional rural/village parish is vastly different from the inner-city parish, the dormitory urban parish, the 'holiday' parish, the recently-created urban parish, the geographically large rural parish, and so on. The detailed pastoral programme of each of these types of parish will be quite different in emphasis and range from the others.

One could list the widely-felt inadequacies of the contemporary parish as follows:

Parish boundaries are outdated and generally have not been redrawn for very many centuries. Even recently-created parishes often seem to be drawn on the basis of fairly arbitrary criteria. Urban parishes usually don't correspond to any natural social groupings. There is very little systematic co-operation between parishes on issues that could be tackled effectively on a co-operative basis; individual parishes and parochial clergy often have impossible demands put upon them. Parishes are not sufficiently linked together and stimulated by intermediate structures (deaneries) or supported by an adequate range of diocesan services; few parish clergy appear to have a positive vision of what a parish could be, seeing it often as little more than a spiritual service station; few parishes have fully implemented the broad and positive vision of the role of the laity in the Church outlined in recent Church thinking. Existing parish boundaries have been interpreted too rigidly and absolutely by individual parish clergy. Within parishes very little discussion or overall planning takes place; an increasing number of people, especially the young, don't identify with the parish or don't see themselves as either contributing to, or gaining from it; while small rural parishes can easily be or become real vital communities, most town and urban parishes are not really communities. The larger the urban parish the greater the anonymity, the more submerged the priests are in a whole range of activities and demands on their time, the more mass-produced the liturgy, the more scattered and diffuse the parish activities. Very few parishes seem, in any real sense, to have taken on board the full range of pastoral insights and proposals of the Second Vatican Council and therefore are not responding in an effective way to the experiences, the expectations and the needs of people today.

The parish and theology
What then is or should the parish at its best be? The parish is not primarily a geographical area, or an administrative unit, but a group of Christians in a particular place seeking to live out together, and pass on to others, the life and vision of Jesus Christ. It is the local realisation of the mystery of the Church and is most fully realised when its members assemble at liturgy and go out from there to bring Christ's peace and care to those around them.

The parish is a localised unit within the Church but it does not stand on its own. It is in fact essentially incomplete, and must be open to the diocese, and to the whole Church, past and present. It must look outwards to its own local community. Its work has to be supplemented at the inter-parochial, diocesan, national and international level.

The parish is a human institution, determined by historical circumstances. Therefore it could be radically altered or even replaced if this were called for. It can take different forms from age to age in particular circumstances.

The task of the parish
It may be helpful to outline in more detail the functions of the parish. There have, in fact, been different attempts to break down the mission of the parish into overall objectives. For example, Avery Dulles has outlined models of the Church which equally apply to the parish life. The five models which he outlined were: The Institutional, that of Mystical Communion, the Sacramental, the Kerygmatic, and the Diaconal. Dulles underlines the importance of 'harmonising the models in such a way that their differences become complementary rather than totally repugnant. In order to do so we shall have to criticise each of the models in the light of all the others. We must refrain from so affirming any one of the models, as to deny, even implicitly what the others affirm.' It is only by a 'combination' of these models that we can come to a full and deep understanding of the meaning of the Church and the role of the parish. It is arguable that it is the failure to do this that has been one of the factors that has contributed to tension as to what the Church should be about, and confusion about the lack of development of the parish system.

The seven functions of the parish which I would isolate are the following. They combine qualities of parish life as well as tasks to be fulfilled by the parish. These clearly overlap but can usefully be separated to underline the major lines of parish life and activity.

(1) Worship
The worship of God is the primary occupation and fundamental duty of the Church. The results of the liturgical changes introduced in the aftermath of Vatican II have been much less dramatic than we were led to expect at the time. On the other hand, the opportunities provided by such profound changes have not been fully utilised. Where the Sunday Eucharist is well prepared and celebrated in a deliberate and personal way, where lay people are involved, where the Prayer of the Faithful, the Offertory Procession and the singing, are imaginative and tastefully executed, and where the sermon relates in a sensitive way to people where they are, then the liturgy can speak powerfully of God, enrich the lives of the participants and create an apostolic spirit. The formality,

dullness and the cold anonymity that people complain about is replaced by a sense of vitality and joyful community.

One of the ways of doing this fairly effectively, in my experience, is through parish liturgy groups. We have such, a small group, working for the past two years in the Gorey parish and it has immeasurably enriched the celebration and the participation at our week-end liturgies.

(2) Formation

The whole thrust of parish life should be to help people grow to full Christian maturity. The liturgy, apostolic groups, parish activities, are focused on the formation of people as much as the explicit programmes of adult religious education and the work of schools. Catechetical development is probably one of the areas of renewal in the Church which has been most successful and has enjoyed very widespread acceptance and impact. It is a good example of how an ideal, properly researched, supported by specialised staff and resources and officially promoted, can be implemented right through the Church.

Adult Christian education is something which the Church considers a priority at the moment. An educated and questioning world needs an educated grown-up faith. Every parish in the country could, without very much difficulty, set up one or other programme of this type. The simplest and easiest staring point is probably a programme linked to occasions such as Confirmation, First Communion, school entry and school leaving. There are also quite a number of highly successful parish-based programmes now in operation, many of them under the aegis of the Maynooth Adult Education Department.

(3) Social and Pastoral Care

One of the basic ingredients of Christian community life from the beginning was a practical care and concern for those in need within and outside the community. Down through history, the parish has had an honourable record of social and community service. Parishes in the past have formed groups to teach, to assist the poor, to protect those who need care. Parochial organisations of workers established labour standards, hours of pay and proper working conditions. In more recent times, parish-based programmes for youth, the elderly and the handicapped have been developed in many areas. Clearly the pastoral care the priest provides (through visitation of the sick and handicapped, the care of young people, counselling and parish visitation) is a striking example of Christian love in many parishes.

In modern conditions, those outside the Church, or on the fringes of the Church, feel very strongly that if Christianity does not issue in practical love for people in need, then it is not Christianity and is worthless.

(4) Challenging Witness

All Christians are called to witness to their distinctive values and life-style. The local parish needs to witness to the Christian vision of life and society as much as the national Church – not just in word but also in the every parish operation. Various committed groups of Christians could spearhead this sort of witness and help the local parish to be an explicit sign of spiritual realities in the local community.

Part of the legacy of the over-identification of the parish with the local community is the inclination not to stand against powerful interest groups or unhealthy developments. Yet more than ever today, people expect the Church to witness to human values and social concern.

(5) Building Christian Communities

The word 'community' is ambiguous and is used in many different contexts. Sociology, theology and liturgy seem to be talking about different things when they use the term. It seems to me that the modern parish can be called a community only in the loosest sense. In trying to decide what we mean by parish community, it certainly is not helpful to use it and 'local community' interchangeably. One of the results of that is that a distinctive parish identity has not developed. One basic fact is clear: Christianity needs a community. If people are to lead a Christian life, they need to be associated closely with others who share their spiritual outlook on life and who can support them in their pursuit of gospel ideals. Perhaps the occasional, very small, rural parish is this sort of community. The vast majority of parishes are not and probably cannot be.

In that event it is probably better to think about the parish in terms of several communities rather than as one undifferentiated community. The vitality of any larger community is manifested through the spread of a number of small communities, and it is through these that the larger community is built up. To use a sociological term, we are talking about setting up more primary groups within the parish, that is, groups where members personally know one another, are involved in fairly regular face-to-face contact, where they share common experiences and a common outlook on a number of things, and where they work together. The family is the obvious and most important primary group and should have a central role in pastoral strategy. But it would be unrealistic to base our whole pastoral approach on the family. Other primary groups of Christians need to be established and supported – small groups of families, Bible study and reflection groups, various social concern groups, groups based on common interest or occupation or neighbourhood, and so on. Such primary groups could be the source of the prayer, formation, and religious support that we all need to strengthen our Christian living. Clearly these groups must not be inward looking, but open to one another and working together. All these groups must be brought into relationship with the parish as a whole, sharing in and contributing to its overall pastoral programme and in particular participating in the parish liturgy.

(6) Missionary Orientation
A primary concern of the Church from the beginning was its passionate desire to share the Christian experience with all humans. The missionary orientation of the Church at all levels is something that has received a renewed emphasis in recent Church policy documents. Parishes need actually to support missionaries from

the parish when they are abroad, helping them to feel that they are a concrete expression of the parish's missionary concern. The missionary apostolate, of course, concerns all members of the Church, lay and clerical, and begins nearer home.

The parish has to reach out to those in their midst who are unevangelised and to those areas of human and social life that have not been animated by the gospel. It has been estimated that there has been a fall-off of something in the region of 15% to 20% in the practising membership of the Catholic Church in this country in the past twenty years or so. The percentage is considerably higher is the younger age group and this must bode ill for the future. Within individual parishes, there are varying degrees of faith and commitment even among those who attend Church regularly.

To please those who are easily satisfied is an easy task. To win those who are doubtful, to serve the needs of those who rarely state their views, to welcome those who are questioning and independent-minded, is the real apostolic challenge. Most parishes today need a major pastoral programme to reach out to those who do not practise and to strengthen those whose faith is at risk.

(7) Administration

It is often said that the Church is over-organised and over-administered. A management consultant would consider it under-administered or at any rate administered in a way that does not adjust easily and effectively to changes of attitude and circumstance.

Administrative procedure should not be suspect. Efficient management, up-to-date premises and facilities, even fundraising, are not inimical to the Church's mission. The problem arises when those become ends in themselves. They are necessary to facilitate and consolidate the work of Church. Efficient, flexible, administrative methods, responsive to people and to change, can be an antidote to institutionalisation rather than a cause of it. Because administrative methods in the past have been so resistant to change, so closed to the reactions of people and so concentrated in clerical hands, they have tended to alienate people and lead to the sort of institutionalisation that is destructive of the faith and the personal and social commitment of people. They need not have this effect.

Administrative leadership of the Christian community is often taken to mean that the priest is a 'Jack of all trades'. He often feels that he should be involved in all decision-making and that anything that has to be done is done by him. This seriously weakens the sense of parish involvement and identity and often leads to unimaginative and shoddy administration.

Of course, one can find parishes where some, or all, of these tasks are being preformed satisfactorily. My basic point is that they are not all being attempted universally or with sufficient urgency, or as part of an overall pastoral strategy. It is not a question of selecting one or more of these tasks of the parish to the exclusion of the others. Each of them highlights a particular dimension of the Church's life and work. It is difficult, but essential, to balance conflicting demands and to work out a personal set of pastoral priorities and working methods which do justice to these varied tasks and which reflect the particular qualities that should mark the role of the pastoral priest.

CHAPTER 6

The Parish and Pastoral Planning

Parish boundaries need to be reviewed and related to more natural social groupings in some areas. This is not as important as what happens within the parish and how much co-operation there is between parishes.

There has not been the degree of research and experimentation with other structures such as team ministries, basic Christian communities, pastoral zones, etc., here as there has been abroad. Briefly, it seems to me that the parochial system needs to be adapted and supplemented. While the parish unit remains the basic structure in the local Church, it must not be seen as a self-sufficient or closed structure, but part of a much more complex structure, with interlocking levels, so that what is now done by individual parishes, is divided up and done by different groupings of parishes.

The diocese is too large and often the parish is too small, for effective pastoral action. Again other things can be more effectively done at the level of a small group of parishes, working together.

Teamwork between clergy in a group of parishes has a lot to recommend it. It could achieve a more uniform and informed approach to pastoral affairs, provide greater specialisation and efficiency, eliminate the isolation, frustration and uneven pressure of work some clergy experience, and promote a new understanding of what the Church is. Priests in surrounding parishes need to meet in an organised way to discuss the pastoral needs of the whole area, and work out common pastoral responses. Similarly, the priests in an individual parish need to meet regularly to review their work, plan systematically, pool information, ideas, and approaches and develop a sense of solidarity and common purpose.

The parish's work needs also to be supplemented. The parish needs to be able to draw on the resources of specialised staff and specialised programmes at deanery and diocesan level. Its mission is supplemented by other specialised ministries within the Church.

The relationship between priests and lay people is a very basic element in any discussion of parish planning. The single, most important, issue in the Irish Church is the involvement of laity actively, and on all levels of the Church's life and work. This is both theologically and administratively essential. There needs to be a serious and comprehensive effort to develop and promote a whole range of opportunities for lay involvement. My experience has been that there is a very large number of people in every parish prepared to get involved in specific tasks if they are approached individually, if the tasks are clearly defined and tailored to suit their situation, if they are involved in the decision on how to complete the task and if they are given some orientation in advance which helps them reflect on their Christian commitment and develop their Christian awareness.

This new approach makes new demands on the priest. It demands patience, humility and a great deal of skill. It is difficult to change from an easier and what in the past was an efficient decision-making system, in which there was no need to seek consensus and no thought of gaining insights and ideas from the parishioners.

Each priest needs a plan, a list of priorities out of which he can make the best use of his time and resources. The planning should take place within the context of this new parish partnership. It needs to involve a very thorough re-examination of methods, approaches, use of time and resources.

Most priests have to spend a lot of time with apostolic groups in the parish. Some long-established apostolic groups have outlived their usefulness and should be replaced. Some others need to be updated and forced to shed a narrow, conservative, inward-looking mentality, more interested in maintaining the unchallenging fellowship of like-minded people and fairly undemanding activities, than being open and outward-looking. Some new apostolic groups need to be encouraged.

All apostolic groups need to be more closely related with each other and more explicitly linked with the overall work of the parish. Most people working in a parish don't have an overall parish approach. We need to look at what the overall priorities are, how difficulties as a whole can be tackled, how all the tasks of a parish can be brought along as a whole together, how our particular work fits in with overall priorities and plan. The particular parish plan is clearly influenced by the traditions, the needs, the strengths and weaknesses, and the expectations and assumptions of people in that parish. Planning can help a priest to cope with his 'workload' in an efficient, relaxed and understanding way. Without planning, we become like a juggler, spinning plates on many canes. We spend all our time running from one plate to the other, just to keep them spinning at once. Without planning, nothing gets properly done and some things of crucial importance are left undone.

A little 'management by objectives' might be useful in deciding what particular work to concentrate on for a particular period of time, reviewing its progress and its relationship to other priorities and planning for another specified period.

Parish planning has to take place within the context of diocesan and national planning.

There are quite a number of agreed ideals which have been the subject of speeches, discussion, conference resolutions in the Irish Church, and still very little real progress has been made on them. I think, for example, of the repeated commitment to the greater lay involvement in the Church; the regular calls for greater inter-

Church dialogue and co-operation; the frequently-expressed need for a more vigorous role for young people in the Church. I would submit that part of the reason for our failure to realise these ideals is that our methodology is defective. We have failed to develop concrete strategies for implementing these ideals (with time-scales, models, etc.); there is not really an adequate system and structure in the Irish Church speedily and effectively to implement these new insights and policies right through the Church.

Pastoral planning is more than just throwing out an ideal. It is guaranteeing that the ideal is implemented: making suggestions, giving guide-lines on how they should be done, providing the resources and personnel to achieve it in an effective, immediate and universal way.

Two pastoral initiatives which have been highly successful by any standards, were the implementation of the new catechetical programmes and the establishment and development of Trócaire. In these cases, a pastoral ideal was simply, quickly and effectively put into practice right through the Church. They were successful, I think, because the following elements were present: a strong commitment to have them implemented; an effective and imaginative planning team at national level; detailed guide-lines were available on procedures and development; there was commitment in each diocese to have something done; and one or more persons in each diocese was given overall responsibility for them.

A basic assumption in this book is that administration is a method by which conscious attempts can be made to ensure that, in every possible way, an organisation is geared effectively to do work it has to do.

Let me mention just three further examples of administrative weakness from the parish level.

(1) Any reasonably sized parish with four priests, with an annual budget of sixty or seventy thousand pounds, may not have a secretary. How many priests use even the basics of adminstration, such as office, filing and records systems, typewriter, duplicator,

computer, annual published financial statement, routine publications, range of working groups, committees, meetings and procedures for assessing progress for the future?

(2) What information, documentation is available to a priest coming to a new parish? Does he even get a clear outline of the parish, its strengths, weaknesses, expectations, traditions etc.?

(3) What precise job description could an individual priest give of his role, covering, for example, such questions as: who do I answer to and in what detail, what tasks am I expected to do, when am I expected to do them, is there a performance level expected of me, how will this be assessed, what resources do I need and from where, what responsibility have I to plan for the future, and so on? I feel the response to each of these would be disappointing.

There is an inbuilt tendency in service/caring organisations, and I would suggest in the Church, for operational initiatives to be located in front line units. Power to decide operational policy remains with individuals or small work groups at the periphery of the structure. They take initiatives on their own, often without reference to superiors. They tend to work independently of each other and there are very real difficulties in establishing direct supervision of their activities. This creates a real dilemma for those who occupy control positions. They are responsible for making policy and maintaining standards, while occupying positions from which this responsibility can least effectively be exercised.

This dilemma can at least partially be solved by strengthening the pattern of operational control and by reducing the autonomy of front line units. These attempts include control through intense professional training which ensures that the front line worker acts in accordance with a given set of norms, even in absence of intense supervision.

Central units can attempt control through the structure of communication, i.e. requests for regular reports, copies of letters and documentation, questioning, 'on-site' collection of information, etc. All these help secure a free flow of upward communication.

Supervision may be intensified by increasing the number of lower level 'inspectors' of one sort or another. Another method is the use of charismatic figures – front line performance is exposed to the correction and advice of particular leaders. Centralisation of financial decision-making, and decisions about the distribution of resources, may also be a useful method of control. At any rate, the parallel with the position of parish clergy in the Church is fairly clear.

Structures

In a hierarchial type of organisation, decision-making is concentrated at certain specific levels within the organisation. According to A.W. Spencer (*Uses of Sociology*) its effectiveness is related firstly 'to the extent of correspondence between the levels at which the problem arises and the levels at which decisions can be made.' If these are far apart, there is not likely to be effective functioning. Secondly, its effectiveness is 'related to the numerical ratio between the superior and inferior leaders on levels below – to the span of responsibility.' If this is too great, the superior cannot control his inferior. On the other hand, the greater the number of authority levels, the greater the difficulty of communication. In a hierarchical organisation, Spencer says:

'The upward flow is "filtered" to make sure it pleases the superior; the downward flow is restricted to ensure that subordinates do not take independent action; sideways information is minimised because of the peer conflict found in hierarchical organisations.'

So a major objective would be to try to keep the span of responsibility low by creating new authority levels, and at the same time avoid the inevitable communication problems that arise from this. The Church has no structures to meet situations created by social change and has so stretched spans of responsibility that bishops cannot effectively exercise control or decision making. The bishop has simply too many subordinates directly responsible to him and is expected to fulfil too many tasks. In fact, impossible demands are made on a bishop because of the weakness of the structure and very often he does not have the range of back-up professional personnel which he needs if he is to be effective, and which he would have in any other agency.

'The function of any administrator is to provide the organisation, or the level he is responsible for, with a well-defined formal structure, to promote co-operative effort amongst its members, to find and deploy resources, and to direct, manage, supervise and evaluate its performance' (*An Introduction to Administration for Social Workers*, Joyce Warham,).

These tasks the bishop is expected to do virtually single handed and, therefore, subordinates largely escape 'his control', except in certain areas of detailed regulation. It also means that the most important types of ultimate control – setting immediate goals, checking performance in relation to goals and development of programmes and services, reviewing and developing policy – is often left undone.

The hierarchical structure needs to be adapted to incorporate a number of effective brackets of command, more specialised ministers and apostolates developed, and a reallocation of responsibilities between the parish, the districts, the deanery and the diocese.

There is another important development which has a bearing on this and has been taken on board by most other organisations and institutions. Increasingly people are participating in and influencing the decision-making process in all areas of life that affect them. It is clearly established that where group participation is found in an organisation, it is more successful in pursuing its goals than one where decision making is exclusively confined in the hands of a few. One of the major sources of alienation from the Church today, in my experience, is frustration felt by people at their inability to exercise influence upon the decisions and the life of the Church. It also results in the prodigious waste of untapped resources. Concentration of power and influence in too few hands means that 'awareness of the extent of problems is too slow and therefore decisions are often not made until they are too late to be effective, or the decisions may betray ignorance of the facts of the situation' (Spencer). People who have participated in the definition of objectives and search for solutions are committed to the implementation of the solution and the pursuit of the objectives. Without that, in modern conditions, any programme or objective, however desirable, is met with and frustrated by varying degrees of mass non-co-operation. So it is of crucial importance that new opportunities exist for participation in the decision-making processes, new structures of dialogue and involvement whereby people's views, expectations, hopes, fears and experiences are communicated to those in positions of influence and responded to by them.

The Brazilian Church structure seems to respond to the need for more participation and more levels of authority. It seems to be a structure of overlapping groups (basic Christian community, parish, deanery, area, diocese, nation, continent). Each group is linked to the one above by one of its leaders. So leaders serve as linking pins to lock the structure together. This overlapping group-structure promotes communication of information, ideas, suggestions and a greater awareness of problems and, above all, a feeling of involvement and motivation. Every diocese has a pastoral co-ordinator, as do many areas and deaneries. There are a number of specialised ministries and inter-parochial staff, programmes and committees.

Commissions and Committees
I have referred elsewhere to the development, in the past two decades, of a large, high-cost and well-staffed set of commissions/committees nationally. The two most serious difficulties about these are that they are not co-ordinated between themselves and they are not linked into the life and decision-making processes of the Church to any real degree. There is a minimum of creative contact and co-operation between them. There is, for example, no general secretary or centralised secretariat. Taken together they represent a great concentration of experiences and expertise, but

they are on the fringe of the Church's life and work. In the Episcopal Conference of England and Wales some years ago, there was a major review and stream-lining of the committees/commissions/councils etc. of the Conference and a new structure has developed whereby the remaining bodies are closely linked together under four departments and a central secretariat.

The Department Heads (Bishops) are members of the standing committee of the Episcopal Conference, which guarantees that their deliberations, proposals and programmes are likely to influence closely and be influenced by the Episcopal Conference agenda. A major review and adaptation of the range and operation of these commissions in Ireland is long overdue. Many of those bodies were set up far too quickly after Vatican II. They need to be coolly examined and ruthlessly adapted and perhaps, in some cases, abolished. New structures that are intended to liberate, often prove quickly to be very resistant to change. There is a clear danger that the pastoral effectiveness of the Church could be held up by a plethora of ineffective and unrelated committees, just as much as it could be by an absence of such groupings. So, in brief, what I am suggesting is a new multi-level, inter-linked structure; the development of a range of new specialised ministries/apostolates/programmes; the offloading of at least some current episcopal tasks to others; the streamlining of national commissions/committees so that they can become the power house of insight/ideas/skills and a major element in pastoral planning and evaluation.

Pastoral Planning
To summarise, the priestly ministry is not only one with varied demands and pressures but it is also vague in terms of detailed job description. There are no real performance standards, no adequate checks or regular supervision, no minimum or maximum hours of work, no immediate realisable targets. For example, one priest could get by with fifteen hours of work a week, another might regularly do a hundred. Obviously neither of these situations is ideal. It remains difficult always to balance the demands

of general ministry with those of specialised groups. Most priests would therefore welcome support, help and broad direction. Within this context, pastoral planning and diocesan pastoral plans could help set the direction, decide the priorities and lift some of the pressure from priests working in parishes.

CHAPTER 7

'Pay, Pray, Obey'

In 1974 the Irish Bishop's Conference held a think-in at Mulraney to look at the big issue facing the Church and to plan a strategy for the coming decade. They isolated the progressive involvement of the laity more and more in the life and work of the Church as the great thrust for the coming decades. This was quite a change from the pre-Vatical II cynical but realistic description of the role of the laity as 'Pay, Pray and Obey.'

For eight years from 1979 I was an advisor to the Irish Laity Commission and one was conscious of the vast failures in information flow, in consultation and in lay involvement.

There are priests who still see themselves as the sole decision makers about the needs of and the developments that take place within the parish. Many of their views (explicit and implicit) about the parish and its role are seriously inadequate. For example, the 'Spiritual Service Station' mentality – we are there to provide Mass and the Sacraments if people want to come; or 'The Independent Republic' mentality where the parish is seen as self-sufficient and complete in itself, not looking outside itself to work with other parishes or avail of the specialised services and resources available at deanery or diocesan level; or the 'My Parish' mentality where clergy take on excessively possessive attitudes to their parish and are reluctant to allow parishioners to share decision-making.

There are also groups of lay people who want only the most minimal contact with or involvement in the Church. I would detect four broad groupings in the Church: The traditionalist group who feel any deviation from the practices or approaches of the past is to be fought against; the utilitarian group want the Church for a few basic services – weddings, Christening, funerals and weekly worship – but want no further involvement; the marginalised who occasionally go to Church but are distanced either socially or intellectually from much of Church life and thought; and the committed and questioning who want a more vibrant and challenging experience of Church.

Overall, my feeling is that a quite large number of laity want the experience of a more vibrant and challenging parish life, in which they can fully participate and where they experience their felt needs being met. There are many clergy who want to facilitate that sort of development and that sort of involvement.

Three things, in my view, hold them back. Firstly there is real confusion abut the nature and extent of lay involvement that is feasible or desirable. The often repeated but misleading phrase, 'The Church is not a democracy', sums up a particular difficulty. In my view, the only valid interpretation of that sentence is that there is a certain core of Christian beliefs and values and ritual which is given for all time and is not subject to change on the basis of some majority decision. In other areas of Christian life and thought and administration, clergy do not have a particular infallible insight or competence which qualifies them to be the final decision-makers. On many specific matters (e.g. education, administration, group work, finance, planning and so on) individual lay people may have much more expertise. In many of these areas, openness, discussion and accountability would be a very positive development indeed. This immediately highlights another more basic problem, i.e. the varying expectation and vision of the Church.

A second difficulty relates to bad experiences, over the past few decades, of specific experiments in lay involvement. Twenty years ago the parish council idea was probably something that was rushed into too quickly, without sufficient thought or preparation and from which too much was expected too soon. Lay people expected too much of priests and vice versa. That left a legacy of some frustration, caution and an unwillingness to move into new forms of lay involvement.

There are situations too where clergy try too hard to anticipate the reactions and the objections of some sections of their parishioners. While prudence and sensitivity to the view of all sections of the parish are important, simply trying to avoid conflict is not adequate justification for always maintaining the status quo. It may be a sure recipe for a dead parish.

The third problem relates to methodology. The Church is simply not good at pastoral planning. The vision statement rightly takes much thought and time, but the other equally important stages are virtually ignored.– setting objectives, developing strategies, agreeing targets, getting structures and procedures right, and reassessing and refining these in the light of experiences. Structures, for example, may be secondary, but they are essential to make adequate and meaningful participation possible.

Lay Involvement: the ideal

As I have suggested earlier, an agreed vision of Church and parish is a basic prerequisite to developing real and effective lay involvement. There is need for a new shared understanding by clergy and laity of the nature of the Church as understood by the Second Vatican Council. Serious spiritual and attitudinal formation and training should be at the heart of every new programme for greater lay involvement in the Church. That would also eliminate some of the tension and confusion that has been associated with some such schemes. The concept of many ministries and gifts united in 'one body', mentioned by St Paul, could serve as a basis for the development of real partnership between clergy and laity at parish level.

The growth in the demand for, and reality of, lay involvement has resulted from a number of factors:
1. The new positive vision of the lay person's role and vocation. There has been very considerable reflection on this during and

since the Second Vatican Council and some experimentation with new methods of making this a reality in Church life.

2. The widening concept of evangelisation, and the greater range of services, programmes and activities demanded, have greatly increased the work load of the ordained ministers.

3. The general pattern of a fall in the number of vocations to the priesthood and religious life.

4. The desire for participation is a feature of every aspect of modern social life. More and more we all seem to influence decision-making processes in every area of life that affects us. Participation means new ideas, creativity and better motivation. Its absence means frustration and alienation and a prodigious waste of untapped resources.

Lay involvement then is theologically desirable, psychologically necessary and administratively indispensable. Consultation and lay involvement and participation cannot take place without some structures. Increasingly a properly established parish pastoral council can be the stimulus for developments on many fronts and the location for real partnership between clergy and laity. Because of the historical concentration of all power and decision-making in clerical hands, the priest has to be the initiator and facilitator of this growing lay involvement which may take a long period of thoughtful and patient experimentation to become a reality. The key catalyst for change and development is the priest. The long-term aim is to have lay people involved in all aspects of parish life and in the process to widen the range of parish programmes and services. In an earlier chapter I outlined a number of key functions/qualities of my ideal parish: my vision of the parish is as a caring and worshipping community challenging in word and work, mature in faith, missionary in outlook and well ordered in the service of the gospel.

Lay Ministries in the Church
Frank Henderson, in *Ministers of the Laity*, gives various classifications of lay roles in the Church including the following:

Liturgical ministries: readers, acolytes, lay ministers of communion (for large assemblies, for communion for the sick and for communities without priests), liturgical music, ushers, artists, parish liturgy committees, diocesan liturgy commissions, preparation for sacramental celebrations, liturgy education and formation.

Spiritual and corporal works of mercy: care of the sick and the aged (medical care, visiting, communion, volunteer services), feeding the hungry, clothing the naked, visiting those in prison, sheltering the homeless, burying the dead, admonishing the sinner, instructing the ignorant, counselling the doubtful, comforting the sorrowful, praying for the living and the dead, leading the leaderless, reassuring the confused, widening horizons, inspiring the young, pioneering in deep waters.

Others: catechists, ecumenism, promoting family life, leadership training, working with youth, education for media, needs of particular groups, spiritual development, art and beauty, creativity, people with serious problems, Christian witness.

So we need vision, new language, new approaches and new struct-ures whereby people can find a deeper faith, a sense of commun-ity, an experience of 'ownership' and the challenge and opportunity to serve in their own parish. All this makes great demands on the priests, especially in the initial period. It demands patience, humility and a great degree of skill. It is indeed difficult for the priest to change to a consultative style of decision-making and team-work style of leadership.

The Parish Pastoral Council: Objectives, Structures, Membership
The parish pastoral council is a grouping that brings together lay people, religious and clergy working jointly to build up the parish as a living Christian community. Let me quote a piece from the Pontifical Council of the Laity in Rome:

Thus parish council members care about parish life in the

other communities of the diocese, share in the concerns of the Church universal, and strive to bring the gospel message to all people and places in their neighbourhood.

Through reflection, planning, animation and action, the parish pastoral council is the place where those ministries or services are brought forth that are needed for the growth of a living parish community. Thus the pastoral council must carefully consider the needs of the faithful and search within the community for the means that will adequately respond to these needs.

This responsibility of the parish pastoral council does not take away from the continued mission and responsibility of the parish as a whole. Each baptised parish member remains responsible in his or her own way for the mission of the parish. In this way the parish pastoral council is a means for implementing better the responsibilities of the whole parish community.

Composition

The parish pastoral council must be representative of the faithful of a particular parish and of various pastoral activities that are carried out within its boundaries.

Without focusing on a false elitism, potential members of parish councils should have certain basic qualifications such as a keen desire to help as well as the ability to listen, reflect and express themselves with care. In other words, future parish council members should be able to communicate and work with others, and to adapt quickly to new challenges.

However, all parish members should learn about the nature and role of the parish council so that interested people may become aware of its various tasks. Finally, the parish pastoral council will make a special effort to help members integrate quickly into their office.

It further recommends that the members of the parish should not be regarded in different ways but goes on to say that as members of the council one should always find women and men of different age groups and civil status (married, single, young, old, employed, unemployed), people from different ways of life or social conditions; people from different geographic sections of the parish; religious (men and women) working or residing in the parish; the parish priest and often the parish clergy.

It says also that the pastoral council should never be a mere federation of movements, committees or other organisations of the parish, but, at the same time, that the principal section of pastoral activities in the parish should be represented.

There were believed, four years ago, to be literally hundreds of parish pastoral councils or parish committees right throughout the country. There are obviously wide differences of approach, achievement and structure. Let me take one example where I think there has been a very successful effort to establish and continue such a council: Mount Merrion in Dublin.

In an article in the November 1987 issue of the *Ferns Diocesan Bulletin*, John Doorly described the objectives and procedures as set out in the constitution:
a) To create an awareness in each parishioner that they had a personal mission in the parish in addition to the Church as a whole;
b) To harmonise the part clergy, religious and laity play within the parish;
c) To relieve the clergy of non-pastoral duties.

Membership of the Council was made up of clergy and religious, representatives of working groups in the parish, nominated members from clubs and social, charitable and prayer groups, and elected members from the parish. Six places were reserved for members under thirty. In all, there were forty-six members.

Nine committees were set up by the parish council. Most of these committees had already been in existence but they were given a more formal structure. All parishioners were invited to attend meetings held by these various committees and at these meetings committees were elected. Membership of committees was not confined to the council members. These committees then prepared their own terms of reference which were subsequently approved by the parish council. He sums up in these terms: 'The position over the past few years shows a general growth in the involvement of parishioners in parish life. There is a continuing growth as a result of the tensions that arise.'

The nine committees and working groups that the council set up and worked through were as follows: finance; property maintenance; parish centre; adult education; social programme; liturgy; communications; community care and youth activities. Each of these devised and carried through a programme of work under the overall direction of the council.

Obviously that sort of structure is not realistic for a small area but it is useful in that it outlines the main task that any parish has to fulfil. Some small rural parish councils don't, for example, break up into any sub-committees. They simply assume responsibility for these tasks through the parish council meetings. Others have a smaller number of sub-committees i.e. (a) Finance and property; (b) Information and communications; (c) liturgy; (d) social and pastoral care. Of course in every case it is important not to assume responsibilities of other existing groups and committees (liturgy, finance, etc.) Ideally these should become sub-committees of the council.

Some Practical Suggestions
To finish this chapter I want to make a few practical suggestions from my own experience, about how the involvement can be increased. My experiences in working in the Social Services Council would suggest points like the following:

(1) Structures and Committees are important.
As I have said, one of the best structures that developed, and is indeed being refined over the last two decades, is that of the Parish Pastoral Council. This sort of group can co-ordinate activities, planning and developments, link people together and help prevent duplication of effort and resources. Common policies and

approach are adopted through the Parish Council and priorities for action are decided. Generally speaking, such a council would also have several sub-committees and special working groups. Through meetings, elections, discussions and the annual general meetings, everyone can have direct or indirect say in decision making. Such a Parish Pastoral Council can then be a concrete example of an individual parish facing its needs and problems, channelling its energy and resources and, in the process, this can greatly improve the quality of life and help the parish develop a sense of identity and self-worth. My own approach is literally to do everything as part of a group, whether big or small, within the parish and I find things are done better, more successfully and are more widely supported for that reason.

There are of course other important groupings in the parish. The new Code of Canon Law, for example, speaks of parish finance committees (Canons 536, 537) and, in my own experience, a Liturgy Group and a Parish Newsletter Committee are structures that can improve the quality of involvement and service in any parish.

(2) Training is very important

People's vision of the Church may be outdated, their approach may be too narrow, and within an individual parish people may be working out of several different models of Church. For that sort of reason, some years ago, the Canadian Laity Commission recommended that the first task of a newly established Parish Council was to undertake a formation course – for example, sessions on the Church, Parish, the role of the laity, and so on. Several lay involvement programmes have, as their first activity, had an extended indepth examination of theology and the gospels.

(3) Public education is important

The Parish Council would set out to inform and to make members of the parish more aware of the Church and its needs and problems.

A system whereby people's opinions are sought and needs are assessed is also very valuable. Wexford town parish, some years ago, did a sort of Parish 'self survey' which resulted in the establishment of the 'Watch – We Are the Church' programme, which was a practical experiment in lay formation, involvement and parish development.

(4) Making choices is important
An American Pastor is quoted as saying that since Vatican II, his parish has become 'a member of the programme of the Month Club'. Every area was recommended as the parish's first priority. There is no end to the new pastoral parish programmes being developed, special needs being highlighted, activities demanded, services recommended, particular groups demanding attention. All this can be bewildering for the priest, especially in a situation where little or no lay involvement is developed or no groups are established. No parish can simultaneously institute developments on several fronts, but they can do them progressively and systematically if they can get the structures in place. This involves making choices between different programmes and activities, and beginning at the process of lay involvement.

(5) Opportunities for voluntary involvement
It's important also, in for example the Social Services area, to develop programmes of voluntary involvement. There are many people in every area who are unwilling or unable to give the permanent commitment to join an organisation. However, they could help on an occasional or once-off basis. As I mention later, a lot of Social Services Councils have initiated volunteer bureaux with public recruitment sessions.

In other cases we approach the individual personally and ask them to do a task or take part in a programme. Personal invitation proves successful. Sometimes I hear people in the Church say there is no one willing to help. I wonder how often this is because they were not informed of the need, were not consulted, were asked in the wrong way, were asked by the wrong people, or simply the range of opportunities was too limited. As always, who does the asking, how the asking is done, is a key element in the likely response. One of the problems that voluntary workers often find, especially those involved in Church activities, is that too much is loaded on them and that once having volunteered they are caught for life. There is no doubt that excessive or unreasonable demands are put on some volunteers. A positive policy of volunteer recruitment means that the load is spread more widely and that people may leave without feeling that they are letting down anyone or that they are abandoning the project.

This is something that needs to be urgently developed. Of course, there are teething problems and some suspicion between the clergy and lay people. With actually working together and working out a problem, their different distinctive roles are recognised and a good working relationship which recognises each other's skills can emerge. Any structure like a Parish Pastoral Council will work only if it is given real scope and clearly defined terms of reference. Anglicans for example, have worked out an interesting set of rules as to what are the areas which are clergy responsibility and what area are lay responsibility.

A Parish Pastoral Council should in my view aim for participatory democracy (where the views of all parishioners are regularly sought and treated seriously) rather than representative democracy where people who are elected just get on with it and make the decisions. Of course the ultimate responsibility lies with the priest, as the full-time trained and appointed leader of the parish. Today we are all finding that the style and exercise of leadership has to change considerably. A priest who is not used to working with groups or lacks committee skills or the hidden skills of exercising your leadership role within it, will find it hard to work in this sort of structure. Having said all that, there is an increasing number of Parish Pastoral Councils. More and more of them are successful and worthwhile. Today they are not only expected by the parishioners but they are encouraged by the Church at the highest level.

PART II

The Church and Society

CHAPTER 8

Beware the Emperor's Embrace

We seem to have great difficulty in Ireland in conducting any debate on socio-moral issues in a calm and reasonable way. As I write this chapter in the aftermath of the Maastrict referendum I am very conscious of the bitterness, the abuse and the totally exaggerated claims that were made by both extremes in that debate. Having said that, the level of bitterness and abuse wasn't as intense or extensive as it was in the 1983 Pro-life amendment campaign or in the context of the divorce referendum three years later.

Two other advances that were noticeable in the most recent referenda were, firstly, the fact that the politicians adopted an all-party approach and this is likely to be the pattern for future debates on issues such as this; secondly, I think the stance of the Church leaders has changed also in that the final statement by the bishops highlighted the issues and factors that they felt should be borne in mind, without actually suggesting how people should vote. This approach was also followed in the statements before the November 1992 referenda. These are definite advances. The 1983 Pro-life amendment campaign was one of the most divisive and disheartening periods that I have lived through as a priest. I hadn't been convinced that there was a need for the referendum in the first instance. The Church allowed itself to be steamrolled by some of the most militant pro-lifers into backing the campaign. (Very many people, including myself, found it extremely difficult to decide how to vote.) I have, however, been struck by the number of people that I met who voted against the amendment and were hurt by things that were said and done by some active supporters of the amendment, including priests.

They objected to things such as sermons for five or six Sundays consecutively on this topic alone, use of Church buildings and grounds for Pro-life canvassers and collections, sermons on Sundays by member of SPUC, sermons which went contrary to the conscience clause in the bishops' letter. Even those most actively opposed to the amendment, in my experience, fully supported the right of the bishops to speak on the issue and felt that the statement was fair, but what they did object to was the way the issue was handled at parish level.

My experience has been that one of the results of that campaign was that abortion, which up to then had been a taboo subject and an option which was rejected by the overwhelming majority of people, was less widely ruled out and less absolutely rejected by people afterwards.

The 1983 and 1986 Referenda, and the public debate associated with them, highlighted inconsistencies in the approach of the Church in different ways. There seemed to be different treatment of priests who took a public stance. Diocesan priests who spoke out in favour of the divorce amendment were apparently instructed by their bishops to take no further part in public debate. But the bishops' statement was not followed through by quite a number of clergy. In many places there was a clear direction from the pulpit as to how to vote.

The message was conveyed that the old issues, the real issues that the Church are concerned about are the sex-related ones. No others are likely to galvanise the Church into action at all levels. It is the one thing on which the Church seems to speak out on with most frequency and urgency and on which all the forces at the Church's disposal are massed. If only the same energy, many people felt, was focused on other issues, such as unemployment and violence, the results could be striking.

I think the debates and campaigns also raised some important questions. There is the question, for example, of competence. In the broad field of Church social teaching, there is a long established tradition that the Church expounds on broad values and principles but does not usually have the competence or expertise or detailed knowledge to comment definitively on a specific application of these principles. For example, the Church expounds on the principles involved in, and the criteria for, just strikes, but it does not usually say that individual strikes are just or unjust. The judgement on the effects of a particular piece of legislation is essentially a legal or sociological judgement. On this, how can the Church have special competence? It seems to me that there has been an implicit confusion between the teaching of the Church and the scientific judgement of the effects of a proposed change.

The weakness of structures and of planning in the Church was again very obvious during these campaigns. There was abuse of the pulpit, when people were told to vote in a certain way, or statements were made which ignored or went beyond the conscience clause in the bishops' statement.

It seems to me that in campaigns of this sort, on moral/political issues, we need detailed ground rules. As I have said earlier, there is no clear structure and procedure for effectively implementing a proposal right through the Church, monitoring its progress, evaluating its success or failure and then refining the approach and methodology. The very same weaknesses were shown up on the occasions of the Divorce Referenda and the Pro-Life Campaign and these weaknesses need a response.

Facing up to the new Right in the Church.
There is and has been, since the late 1970's, an organised campaign by a sinister combination of the Right to tighten its control of the Church. One has only to look at some of the supposedly Christian Journals which appeared over the last decade and see the vicious attacks on health education programmes, catechetics, CMAC, reputable theologians, Trócaire, to realise this. It was quite dangerous, it seemed to me in the 1983 Pro-Life campaign, that the Church and politicians were steamrolled into the cam-

paign in quite a short period of time, with the running been made by a very small group indeed.

The referenda also faced us with the question, what should be the relationship between Christians and society and its politics? Traditionally there have been some distinct but overlapping models as follows:

The Christian Society
The Church tries to gain control and govern society. Not only does this model provide (at least in theory) the nearest possible approximation to the perfect rule of God, but the world is also governed in a way that harmonises with the growth of the Christian Church. Such a strategy blossomed after the Roman Emperor Constantine made the empire Christian. The danger of such a model is that the Church becomes obsessed with power and abuses and 'witch hunts' can easily develop.

A Christian Alternative
In this model, the people of God do not seek to govern society. Rather they aim to show a distinct alternative community, to be a sign of the Kingdom, bearing witness to priorities and values different from those furthered by the ruling group. It is hoped thus to attract people to the values of God and his salvation and thereby to affect the world both by example and by increasing the numbers of Christians in society at large. This seems to me to be the de facto position adopted by Churches widely to-day, and especially successfully in Latin America. It also seems to fit in well with St Paul's encouragement to concentrate on apostolic teaching and developing a Christian lifestyle. This position is one which is respectful of secular authority. The two great dangers of this approach are that the world is shunned or largely ignored, and believers can fall into arrogant self-righteousness.

A Christian Withdrawal
The extreme version of the alternative model finds that, since the world is 'evil', the only basis of hope is to separate from society as completely as possible and await a direct intervention of God.

Attempts to participate in political decisions-making are seen as pointless. (This is the strategy of the Jehovah Witnesses).

A Christian Leavening
In the parable of the leaven in the lump, Jesus taught that the coming of the kingdom of God would affect the whole world. Christians are to promote the growth and purity of the kingdom and justice in society at large without seeking to rule that society. But there is a danger that one too easily accept society as it is without challenging or criticising in a radical way. (Christians must fulfil a prophetic role and pressure for effective action.)

To-day I feel we should be moving from the Christian society model to one that combines the alternative and leavening models.

For example, in his statement before the Divorce Referendum, Bishop Comiskey of Ferns said:

> I, for one, hope that the compassion much mentioned in this debate by both sides will find practical expression on the part of Church and State in preparing for and supporting the institution and Sacrament of marriage. There is a life after the Referendum.
>
> Problems remain and there is one which contributes enormously to the breakdown of family life. I refer to the continued unemployment of literally hundreds of thousands of Irish men and women and the emigration by stealth of some of the best and brightest of our youth. Would that all the parties involved in this debate devote the same passion the same energy and the same commitment to this greatest of problems facing our country.
>
> Young people have been the target of many appeals during the past few weeks. If prelate, priest and politician, canvasser, and campaigner, returned to the secure fortress of our own employed, then the only winner of Thursday's vote will be cynicisim.

The Family

It is important to remind ourselves that the family in Ireland or amongst the Irish abroad is strong and resilient and is accorded the greatest status and importance. Legal supports and safeguards to the family have a role but I am convinced that the Irish family can, without difficulty, survive and indeed flourish even in neutral or non-supportive environments because of its inherent strength.

The family is clearly the most important group with which any individual has associations during his lifetime. It is the group whose influence begins earliest and lasts longest; the only group into which he is received without any choice on his part; the group which has the widest expression of age differences and the group in which emotional ties are the most intimate and lasting.

I have a profound suspicion about the approach, the attitudes and the sense of gloom of some of those who proclaim themselves defenders of the family against real or imaginary attacks. When they are seen to be doing something concrete in a specific, immediate and comprehensive way to help and support real families being undermined by poverty, unemployment, breakdown of relationships, lack of opportunities and services, they can speak with credibility and effectiveness. Many of those who shout the loudest and the shrillest lack conviction and authenticity.

While it is perfectly right that Christians should stand for and campaign for social values and the kind of society that they believe in; this must always be done calmly, reasonably, openly and honestly. The axiom 'Truth without love is cruel; love without truth is sentiment' is of great relevance in this context.

While the teaching of the Church is very clear on various family related issues, it does not necessarily follow that the state should incorporate all these in legislation. The Emperor's Embrace can and has been dangerous for the Church and its values, and excessive dependence on laws to uphold moral beliefs can have the opposite effect to the one intended. At base, it is the family itself that provides confident values, moral standards and the ability to live with and relate to others. The most important role of the State is to provide the widest possible range of specific services, resources and personnel to reinforce the family's functions and potential.

We are sometimes too easily panicked by changes that appear to work against Christian values and over-react in a hysterical and offensive way which prevents us from winning hearts and influencing minds, which is the only way in a democracy that one can influence legislation. Some changes clearly do work against Christian values. But if there were to be growing public and legal acceptance of situations which Christians were opposed to, all is not lost. There is a new opportunity which demands faith and hope – a new opportunity to witness.

It might well be that Christians have a great chance to make clear the true humanness of moral standards that had come to be seen by many people to be arbitrary and cruel. Because child bearing is sometimes regarded as an optional extra, because divorce and living together outside marriage carries less social stigma, then maybe Christians have a new opportunity to bear witness to the truth in a totally new situation. We can show that children matter because they are themselves, not because they suit our conveniences. We can show the growth of a family is for the spiritual development of all its members. Greater public acceptance of divorce could allow an opportunity for the value of Christian love and fidelity in marriage to be shown in a new light because it is not imposed by convention but inspired by faith.

As I've said, what is of even more crucial importance than legislation underpinning particular moral values are supportive programmes and services that help strengthen families and allow them fully develop their potential. The Christian family down through the centuries has survived and blossomed in the most unpromising circumstances. There is much too much gloom in this context. An act of faith and an affirmation of the family is overdue.

CHAPTER 9

No Sacristy Priest

There has been in Ireland, a long and honourable tradition of involvement by the priest in helping build up the community and develop services of one sort or another for the needy. The sacristy priest, concerned only with the Church and 'Churchy' things, has definitely not been an Irish phenomenon.

I am convinced that the still high level of commitment to the Church, and the general respect and trust which is given to priests, is related to that fact. When I was a student in Maynooth that tradition was held up as an ideal. Indeed it was given increased strength by the general mood of the decade. The sixties began a period of rapid and generally welcome social change and increased tolerance, widespread social awareness, greater involvement and social concern. To have been young and a student in the late 1960's was a tremendously stretching experience. We felt that we could change things. We felt that we were our brother's keeper. It was a time for rediscovering the social dimension of Christianity.

The Christian vision is still strong, and could be harnessed towards the task of creating a genuinely Christian society. The basic test of a Christian society is the extent to which, both in statutory and voluntary provision, it helps those who are underprivileged and deprived, whether physiologically, educationally, socially, or physically. Christ said that love should overturn the world. A whole new set of relationships must exist between people. They must treat others with affection and respect. No person must call another inferior because he speaks with the wrong accent, has the wrong colour of skin, wears the wrong clothes or lives in the wrong area. People must share the goods of the earth with others. Those who are sick in hospital or in prison must be visited. Those who are strangers, with different attitudes, practices or behaviour, must be welcomed. Those who have nothing to give must be given to. Those who are weak must be fought for. How does Ireland, as a society that claims to be Christian, live up to this? It is still the ideal that as Christians we are working towards and the vision that motivates quite a few people.

Social and Community Services

This vision generated a huge development of social services and community initiatives right across the country, including special services for the elderly, youth programmes and clubs, the development of schools and occupations for the disabled, services and agencies for travellers, child-care facilities, special services to aid marriage and the family, improved opportunities for the mentally sick, and so on. There was a huge increase in the level of voluntary involvement and a recognition that the obligation to love your neighbour to-day involves joining or forming organisations or agencies that aim to improve the quality of community life.

Committed clergy and laity were to the fore in these developments – people like Bishop Peter Birch, Erskine Childers, Fr James McDyer were among those who inspired and led these developments.

One of the areas in which I have been actively involved for the past eighteen years or so, is the Community/Social Services Council Movement. I want now to outline the background to these developments.

In a town of any size in this country, there are a number of organisations which are concerned in one way or another with the quality of life. Some are Welfare organisations concerned with the elderly or disabled people needing help with their day to day living. Some have been formed by neighbours who have joined together for leisure-time activities or to run youth clubs or ladies' social clubs or play groups for young children. Others are involved in the whole range of sporting, recreational or cultural activities. Various statutory local and regional authorities provide many important services, ranging from health, housing and so on to street lighting and refuse collection. And there are other statutory authorities who work through local offices. All these and many more contribute to the life of the town and directly or indirectly affect the lives of its citizens.

These organisations and authorities have specific functions. Public authorities have these defined by law and voluntary organisations have them determined by their constitutions or terms of reference. Yet many situations and social problems cannot be solved by one of these alone but only by joint consultation and joint action; nor can the total needs of community be completely met by the work of individual bodies providing particular services. There is a need for a more broadly-based representative body with a concern for the well-being of the town/community in which they live, to plan and develop social policy, initiate new services and improve and extend existing ones. Constructive and broader social thinking of this kind, over the last three decades or so, has led to the development of Social Service Councils, Community Councils, and Community Services Councils.

These are the three broad types of Council which operate in different parts of the country and there are over three hundred of them in the Republic. It is not easy to distinguish clearly between their objectives and activities, but, generally speaking, they can be distinguished in the following ways: Social Service Councils are usually councils representative of voluntary organisations in an area and they work together in the provision of social services. The Community Social Service Council is somewhat broader in membership and scope, involving voluntary groups but also representative in some way of the people in an area and assisting, improving and increasing existing services in an area. The Community Council, on the other hand, is representative of the people and organisations of an entire area, concerned with improving the overall quality of life in the area, frequently trying to provide Social Services but basically concerned with the development of the Community in all its aspects. One of the most striking differences between Social Service Councils here and in Britain is that local statutory agencies in Britain are actively involved as full members in the activities and programmes of the councils.

Social Services Councils emphasise that they are not separate organisations and do not interfere with the automony of member groups. They consist of the organisations that make them up. Decisions are made democratically by representatives of all the groups. The most important feature of them is that they are based in, established by, and closely related to, the local community.

The widening and making more sophisticated of the range of personal social services has largely been associated with the development of these councils. They were concrete examples of individual communities facing the needs and problems of their own community and channelling their energies and resources to help themselves. This has improved the quality of life in many local communities and helped the community to develop its feelings of self worth and retain power over its own community life. (Statutory services, however extensive and effective, cannot provide this sort of community development). Many communities responded quickly to the challenge involved in the establishment of Social Services Councils and, from within their own areas, provide the resources needed to develop programmes.

New needs emerged and new services developed and staff was employed to meet these needs. A changing emphasis on the family led to a greater family orientation to social work diagnosis and treatment. Perhaps most astonishing of all was the facility with which numbers of communities responded and the wide range of developments on various levels which were initiated. All this was not without effect on the statutory services where a new willingness to examine social needs and social welfare was slowly becoming apparent and an impetus was given to statutory agencies to develop services and assist the work of voluntary agencies.

Among the essential roles of a Social Service Council are:
(1) To co-ordinate existing activities;
(2) To identify gaps which are not or will not be met by existing services and to do something about them;
(3) To disseminate information and facilitate communications within the community;
(4) To create a structure whereby the voice of the community can be heard. In any small town a council can bring together Vincent de Paul, Credit Union, Adult Education, Youth Groups, I.C.A., Community Development, Handicapped Organisations, Pre-school Playgroup, A.A. Group, Council for the Blind, I.S.P.C.C., Old Folks, Legion of Mary, Red Cross, Itinerant Settlement, and a number of others. Obviously all this activity does not happen by the mere setting up of a Social Service Council. It takes much time to make this objective a reality in any community.

Clearly there are weaknesses and problems in the organisation and activities of many councils. It is my purpose in this chapter to highlight the positive developments that have taken place and suggest some of the supports etc. that are needed for councils to achieve their objectives. Sylda Hayes, former Development Officer of the then National Social Service Council, listed, ten years ago, three essential elements which need to be available if Councils are to do that: Professional guidance from people competent in community work; an informed and co-operative public so as to guarantee sustained voluntary effort; and interested and co-operative statutory bodies.

These councils represent an effort to widen the range of people involved in social and community work, and are based on the belief that locally-based services are more effective and that voluntarily-provided services have a special flexibility, relevance and a personalised quality. They represent a new, more positive, open and vibrant approach to need, and a new sense of community.

It is worth outlining some of their features.
1. The Social Services Council Movement was an attempt to return to and re-fashion the pre-Industrial Revolution emphasis on

the local community as the people who cared for their own needs. In the Social Services area a key concept is that of community care. In general, this is taken to mean care in one's own home, contrasted to that given in an institution. The beneficial effects of this policy in the care of the elderly, child care, care of the handicapped, the mentally ill and so on, are very clear. Perhaps a more important meaning contained in the phrase Community Care is this: The whole local community has the obligation of caring for those in need.

The implementation of this concept has already borne fruit in the huge increase in the number of people now involved in community service of one sort or another, and the dramatic increase in local voluntary funding over the past twenty-five years. It has also meant a move from 'charitable' work being the exclusive preserve of the few to the whole local community seeing it as their responsibility. The quality of local Community life improved in the process.

2. The Social Service Council also has begun slowly to create a cooperation between statutory and voluntary organisations. One aspect of this has been the growing co-operation between the full-time trained personnel and the part-time generally untrained volunteers. Initially there were 'teething problems' and some suspicion of each other's motives and competence. With actually working together, and working out in practice their different distinctive roles, a new respect has built up between professional and volunteer and a recognition of each other's special strengths has emerged.

3. When we began Gorey Social Services Council over eighteen years ago, we had no clear blueprint and we could not have because communities, their needs and concerns, are different. We were very unsure of what exactly we were doing, other than trying to do more effectively what we already were doing and to do some new things together. We could never have predicted the range of activities that we became involved in, the scope of the service that we provided, and the number of the programmes we initiated.

New needs emerged and we responded to them. A greater awareness of the range and depth of problems emerged. Perhaps most astonishingly of all was the way in which the local community responded and which made possible the initiation of a wide range of developments. In our most recent Annual Report there are a total of thirty-one projects, events, services etc, which the council is now involved in. There is nothing exceptional about this and the majority of councils around the country could report the same experiences.

Voluntary organisations have historically been very effective at pioneering work which the State may take over later. In some circumstances they work with statutory agencies to provide a community service: They may do work which statutory organisations cannot effectively do or simply are not doing, and they can act as pressure groups with regard to social needs and problems. At any rate, the overall point is very clear. It started out with a simple vision - greater community co-operation and involvement, and with no clear blueprint. The achievements were worthwhile, even if unforeseen or unexpected. Of course there were tensions, problems and failures as there will always be in any new development, but we worked through them and the overall results were very positive indeed.

4. Some of the specific tactics used by Social Services Councils are worth mentioning because they may be helpful as guidelines to those involved in developing any community or indeed pastoral initiatives.

a) Assesssment of needs/opinions
It is clearly of great importance to continually assess very carefully, and on the basis of accurate and detailed information, the types and extent of need, the situation of individual groups, the overall community reaction to projects, and so on. Many councils (often as their launching project) have initiated a community self-survey. This is a survey by members of the community themselves which tries to build up a picture of community needs, inter-

ests and priorities from the views and wishes of each member of the community.

b) Voluntary Involvement.

Community Care also involves the task of encouraging an increasing number of people to become involved and providing opportunities for them to do so. Despite the dramatic increase in the number of new groupings/committees established, and in the number of people who are involved in these and in special projects, there are still many people in every area who are unwilling or unable to give the permanent commitment of joining an organisation but who are willing to help on an occasional or once-off basis. For this reason we, like a number of other councils, initiated a volunteer bureau and volunteer recruitment sessions. In Gorey town, with a population of four thousand people, the first volunteer recruitment session attracted fifty-four new volunteers in response just to a public announcement. In the intervening time, the total number who have volunteered has risen to three hundred and sixty-one Help was offered in the following ways: baby-sitting, home visits, hospital visitation, typing, book-keeping, fundraising, painting, delivery of meals, cooking, sewing, carpentry, providing transport and so on.

We have also experimented with a Good Neighbour Scheme. The basic idea behind the scheme is to have 'contact' people in each area to inform residents about the council and its services, to allow residents to approach that person for information or help, to inform the council of problems and needs, and to ask for care for someone who is sick.

There is one final aspect of voluntary involvement that is extremely important and that is the involvement by younger people in community service and in Church life. There has undoubtedly been an increase in recent years in the interest shown by young people in giving service to the community. We have particularly tried to provide a range of more varied, imaginative and flexible opportunities for involvement by young people and by and large this has been fairly successful.

Again I think that these experiences of increasing the level of voluntary involvement could well be used in increasing the level of lay involvement in the Church.

c) Training and Public Education.

We have always tried to provide a range of training and orientation sessions for volunteers and committee members. Volunteers need to be helped to become more sensitive and skilled in their work with people. As well as this, most members of voluntary organisations need to get advice on how to work on committees, how to organise a service, how to create a good public image, how to keep accounts and present a budget, how to run a meeting effectively, how to broaden resources and so on. Our council has provided a wide range of seminars, workshops, training sessions, discussions, etc. and I feel that it was a key element in the success we have had.

The related area of public education we see as crucially important, In the past, charitable organisations have fought shy of publicity. Their reasons for this were mainly related to the need for confidentiality, but it had the result of leaving the community often genuinely unaware of the extent of poverty and need and reluctant to come forward to help. So public education on attitudes to the deprived, knowledge of opportunities for involvement, and awareness of the types and extent of need, is important. Seminars, exhibitions, publications and regular and substantial press publicity was the way we tried to undertake this programme of public education.

d) A Social Services Centre.

In many of the larger towns, Social Centres have been established to serve as a focal point and base for activities, providing activity and meeting rooms, bookeeping, typing and duplicating services. Full-time staff work from there and contact and co-operation between different groups who use the Centre has developed.

e) The Social Service Council/Committee.

This is the group that co-ordinates activities, plans new developments, links groups together, and helps prevent duplication of effort and resources. Progressively a common policy is adopted and priorities for action are decided. The council has several sub-committees and special working groups and the committee are fully accountable for all activities and decisions. Through meetings, elections, discussion, and AGM's everyone can have a direct or indirect say in decision making.

There are a number of other aspects of the work of Social Services Councils worth mentioning, which also represent difficulties:

Partnership with statutory groups
Voluntary Community Enterprise represents an important aspect of Irish Social Life. This is something quite unique and particularly valuable that Ireland has retained and which is envied by community workers and social planners in other European countries. However, closely planned, adequately financed and wide-ranging voluntary/statutory co-operation is not a marked feature of Irish Life, as it is in Britain for example. Statutory and voluntary action are not the antithesis of each other. They spring from the same roots, are designed to meet the same needs and have the same motivating force behind them. It was Lord Beveridge, one of the architects of modern social policy in Britain, who said 'State action is voluntary action crystallised and made universal.' Broadly speaking, voluntary/statutory co-operation in this country is not common practice. It is a general theory only occasionally applied and often on an uneven and unco-ordinated basis. The need for a Personal Social Services Act which would, amongst other things, offer guide lines and principles in the area of voluntary and statutory co-operation is long overdue. At a local and regional level, a memorandum of agreement between voluntary and statutory agencies, covering for example a period of five years and indicating the role which both will provide, and the relationship between them, would be extremely valuable. It is only in this way that Social Services Councils can develop a permanent and secure role for themselves and actualise their full potential.

Adequate financing

Under Section 65 of the 1953 Health Act, grants are made available to Social Service Councils to help them develop new services and maintain existing ones. Many councils are not happy with the present arrangements although more time needs to be spent on book-keeping and accounts and some councils need to make a bigger effort at their own fund raising activities. A matter of serious concern to all councils are their periodic overdrafts and their relative uncertainty about the budgeting process in general. Councils would welcome an agreed and uniform set of guidelines in all regions for grant-making to Social Services Councils:

(1) A simple standard form of application and timetable for applications, the Health Board Budget, and the Payments of Grants.
(2) A clear and comprehensive list of the types of services and projects which are considered under section 65 grants.
(3) The Services that are considered a priority and the percentage of grants available for these and others.
(4) A more long-term indication of the funding available over a five year period.
(5) A clear indication of the grant aid available for employment of full time staff.

This should greatly assist Councils in planning properly for the future.

In a survey some years ago the average national percentage of their budget raised by Social Service Councils is in the region of 42%. Councils usually have to raise quite a substantial sum in any year. Like all co-ordinating bodies, they have special problems to face when planning fundraising because they cannot compete with their members' organisations. Usually councils concentrate on one or two major fundraising events in any year.

Building up communities

Community care too involves building up of a sense of community knowledge, of identity with and pride in one's local community. Clearly this is an overall objective which is gradually achieved over a long period and which is stimulated by the achievement of some of the other more immediate objectives. Many Social Services Councils have initiated local newsletters as an effort to achieve a greater sense of community. In building up links between different sectors of the community, a number of councils have also established contacts with members of the local community who are abroad, through newsletters, and annual re-unions in English cities.

I have tried to sketch some aspects of an exciting development over the last twenty-five to thirty years in this country, much of it related to the development of Social Services Council. I have also tried to suggest ways in which these can be taken further. One of my strongest feelings in this context is that Christian charity must become more business-like. Feeble good will or pious hopes for a better future are of little use. We need to be much more thorough and professional and we need more research into the types and extent of problems. We need to isolate real problems and our attempts to meet them must be planned and systematic.

Facing the real questions

To accept responsibility for people's welfare in the community, rather than allow them to go to an institution, is indeed a heavy responsibility. Very easily we set up a service or a range of services and presume that because they were fulfilling the needs of the 60's and 70's and 80's that they are also fulfilling the needs of the 90's. There is an interesting parallel to this in Britain. As mentioned elsewhere, in 1965 the Salvation Army produced a report which shocked public opinion in the U.K. 'Tragedies of Affluence' discovered that there were approximately 675,000 elderly people neglected. The structures for helping seemed to be there and in theory no one was in want or neglect.

Have we in Ireland responded adequately to the new social changes, and consequently the new problems and difficulties these have thrown up? Is it not amazing in a Christian society that nobody seemed to have seriously questioned the assumption that economic recovery was a prior condition for a better deal for the poor? A situation of widespread poverty, especially arising from extensive unemployment, should logically mean that the State increases the money available for social welfare payments and for the work of caring organisations who are faced with an unprecedented level of need and requests for help.

Within a free society it is generally agreed that every person has certain basic rights which are recognised by law and various services and provisions are made available so that those needs may be met. Yet there are always people in the community who, for one reason or another, are unable to take advantage of its amenities. They may be too uneducated to know about them, or not in a position to demand them. They may be sick or incapacitated. They may be unable to find work. They may need care and protection because they are young or old or mentally weak. It therefore becomes the duty of the community to help them so that they can share in the amenities which other people enjoy. Our Social Services arise, both voluntary and statutory, to help such people to reach an equality with other people in sharing in the general amenities of the community which are the right of all.

All our charitable caring efforts are based on this ideal of simply giving people their rights so that they can take their rightful place as the equals of the rest of society. There are many pressures and tendencies fighting against the achievement of this ideal. Much more selfishness and prejudice exists today which makes our task so much harder.

In brief, I am saying that our services for the deprived are not nearly as extensive as we think. They can often be selective and intolerant. They are in constant need of wideranging re-examination. They need to be dramatically extended and more generously endowed, especially in the context of widespread unemployment. In trying to do this, we have to fight against prejudice and vested interest which misrepresent the extent of need and actively resist advances.

Some specific examples of caring
I want to conclude this chapter with some specific concrete ways

in which we can become more caring. Care is about the effort we make to understand one another. Care means presence – when you speak, the person knows you are speaking to them; when they speak, they know you are listening to them and not wondering about your possible answer.

Ordinary contact: visiting

One particularly urgent contemporary social problem is loneliness. Today the individual possesses greater opportunities for mobility, for social life, for communication with others than ever before in the history of mankind. Unfortunately, it is all too easy for the individual to sink into isolation and insignificance in the face of the modern impersonal social machine we have created. New forms of loneliness today include the loneliness of retirement, the loneliness of those tied to the house, the loneliness of some children under school age, loneliness of wives whose husbands spend too little time at home, the loneliness of those living alone, the loneliness of young people coming to live in a city, the loneliness of the unemployed and the weekend loneliness of single people.

Many of these people are cut off from others through circumstances over which they have little, if any, control. Keeping in contact, setting up opportunities for people to be in contact with others, and organising regular visits to people who are alone, are of greater importance than ever before today.

Listen and counsel

In a whole range of areas of life today there is an over-riding need – the need for skilled listeners and counsellors. I would like to see, above all else, in every area a full-time supportive, skilled counsellor. Maybe over a period it is something that the Churches together and voluntary groups could aim at providing. The bereaved need this sort of professional service often. So do people faced with other emergencies or crises in their lives – cancer, loss of sight, suicidal feelings, loss of job. Above all, this service would be valuable for marriage counselling, with increased marriage breakdown, much higher expectations of the marriage relationship, greater pressure and demands, greater willingness and ability to verbalise anxieties and concern. There is the need for a more caring, a more accessible and more professional counselling service for all these.

Obviously this can be partly met, and is being met through, for example, CMAC in the area of Marriage Counselling. What I am suggesting is that a more comprehensive and structured response is needed and that it is a very immediate and tangible area of caring.

Set up a caring group
In the last thirty years, as I have said, there has been truly an explosion of community and caring groups. The overwhelming majority of these have been in towns and large villages. There are gaps in services for people outside these. I believe there is a need in every rural community for a caring group who will help to mediate service from the towns to people in their area, who will serve as a listening ear in their community and organise some general services for the elderly, children etc. This would be an important method of making a reality of the concept of Community Care.

CHAPTER 10

Groups with Special Needs

There are some groups whose needs are so great that they need special attention. I will highlight five:

a) Emigrants
Much has been written recently about the problems associated with emigration and the services that are needed to respond to it. I will describe the efforts we have made in a small town parish (population 4,000) in Gorey, Co. Wexford. There is much that can be done at parish level and I believe that services to emigrants will only be fully effective if they are parish based.

I estimate that approximately 7% of the population has emigrated from Gorey since 1980. The overwhelming majority are young people and virtually all have gone to London and Southern England, with 12 going to Australia, 24 to Canada and U.S.A. and up to 20 to the Netherlands. At our Annual Gorey Reunion, which we have been holding in London for the past eighteen years, I get a general feeling of the situation of Gorey emigrants. Compared to emigration in the 1950's there are some significant differences in emigration 1980's style. Younger emigrants today, perhaps reflecting the improved standard of education, seem to have access to a wider range of job opportunities. Emigration is much less a total break with home, than it was – many telephone home twice a week and visit home, in some cases a number of times a year. A very large number of young emigrants from Gorey go to people they know, either friends who have emigrated recently or to more long-term emigrants who have done well in Britain. Linking in to the network of Gorey people who have been successful in Britain is a tremendous boost to young emigrants, and the Parish Reunion in London can facilitate this linkage. This is not, of course, to suggest that all young emigrants do well. There are adjustments and social difficulties for quite a few of them, along with loneliness, unemployment and financial problems.

In responding to emigration, I have found that the most effective way of structuring our efforts was to work through an established community group, which in this case was Gorey Social Services. This guarantees continuity and organisational structure and access to resources. Two immediate services that we try to provide are information for intending emigrants and continuing contacts with those who have emigrated.

Information
It is generally agreed that one of the greatest needs is for information and preparation for intending emigrants. Youth organisations, in recent years, have done much in providing information for intending emigrants and their parents. One national youth organisation with which I have been involved, The National Youth Federation, offers a very valuable advice and information service to young people contemplating emigration, through its regional offices.

For example, I have visited Waterford and Clare Regional Youth Services and saw an imaginative, effective, professional and full-time service of this sort. In Gorey we received a grant from the County Wexford Youth Trust (The fundraising area of the Ferns Diocesan Youth Service) to develop an information programme for those contemplating emigration. We established a special subcommittee, representative of teachers, the parish youth worker, the Unemployment Centre, as well as the Social Services Council, to carry through the information programme.

The elements in this programme were as follows:
1. Information available each working day during normal office hours in the Youth Office and Unemployment Centre to help potential emigrants make an informed and responsible decision.

2. Purchasing supplies of relevant documentation for the Youth Office and the Unemployment Centre.
3. A special information evening on the first Wednesday of each month in the Youth Office, from 8.00 pm to 9.00 pm. This is intended for young people considering emigration and their parents.
4. Information sessions in post primary schools for senior classes.
5. A poster campaign in all places within the catchment area of Gorey, advertising the programmes.

This programme is based on the idea of towns developing services for the outlying rural areas. Alternatively, a rural parish could invite the local ICA or Legion of Mary, or some other community group, to select someone who could get some general training and offer emigration information on a specified evening once a month or by appointment. Whatever form it takes, young emigrants need easy access to information and advice that can help them make informed decisions and be adequately prepared.

Continuing Contact
Gorey Social Services Council has tried to maintain contact with Gorey people living abroad in three ways:

Twice Yearly Magazine
We produce a twice yearly magazine, with local sales covering the production and postal costs of sending over 300 copies to Gorey people abroad. The feedback that we get suggests that this is much appreciated and eagerly awaited by emigrants as a way of keeping in contact with news and developments at home. In drawing up a mailing list, members of the Youth Club called to all houses in the parish collecting names and addresses of emigrants. This list is updated every two years and new names are regularly handed in to us.

Annual London Re-Union
We have a well established Annual Reunion of Gorey people in the London area. Each year we send an invitation to each person/family on our magazine mailing list and we try to get good publicity, well in advance of and after the Reunion, in the local papers.

We usually arrange to have photographs taken at the Reunion to be printed in the local papers. Up to the early 80s we had an average attendance of about 100 at the Re-union. After that the numbers grew steadily and two years ago reached an all time high of almost 300, with up to 100 of those in their late teens or early twenties. It has fallen off dramatically recently as have several other Reunions and we are relaunching it again. We have found the Irish Centre in Camden Town an ideal venue and staff are most helpful in facilitating our plans. For the first five years, the Reunion took the form of a dinner dance. This created problems because, despite our best efforts, it was virtually impossible to have accurate numbers of attendance. Since then, we have a dance and the Irish Centre offers a menu from which people can order as they arrive. The Re-union has always been a happy and nostalgic occasion with old friendships renewed, new contacts made and conversations going on long into the night.

Welcome Home Festival

Each year, in early August in Gorey, there is a ten day Community Festival and we have tried to make this a 'Welcome Home' Festival for returning emigrants. I find that, when the dates are known well in advance, quite a few families arrange to be home on holiday during that period. They are guaranteed a time of celebration, activity and community spirit and a very special welcome. In smaller communities it is possible to have a simple special event of welcome during the holiday period.

We have not done anything extraordinary. However, we have highlighted the need for an information service and a programme of keeping in contact and that every single community can respond in one way or another to the needs of emigrants.

b) Handicapped

Handicapped people are too often seen as 'patients' and 'problems'. They are individuals with the same needs, same emotions and basically the same potential as the rest of the community. A handicapped person has all the same needs as the ablebodied and they have them at the same time. Most disabled people in this country have the ability to support themselves and to make a useful contribution to society. They do need special help and a very special kind of love – a love that can see beyond the surface disabilities and defects to the person beyond. The disabled are not a burden to be borne in charity but unique individuals who need to be helped to develop to their own full potential. Attitudes to the disabled might be much more healthy and accepting if we realise that any definition of disability is a matter of placing an arbitrary borderline through a continuum.

To function as well as possible, disabled people need a range of services of one kind or another.....technical aids, special education and training, medical and vocational rehabilitation, special work opportunities and some organised leisure time activities. This was the sort of thinking that led Gorey Association for the Handicapped to examine, during the late 1970's, ways of making some broadly based full-time provision for the needs of the handicapped of the Gorey district.

More immediately, two particular pilot projects gave a greater sense of urgency to our efforts and pointed them in a particular direction. For the previous four or five years, eleven disabled people had attended a craft session/social afternoon, sponsored by The Association for the Handicapped under the direction of a local nun assisted by a team of dedicated voluntary helpers. For over three years, Gorey Community Development Group had organised swimming lessons for the handicapped in Courtown during the Summer. Both these projects had been remarkably successful and the progress made by the enjoyment given to the handicapped had been quite striking. This confirmed the feeling of the Association that some more permanent provision for the handicapped should be made in Gorey.

The experience and achievements of the County Wexford Community Workshop Ltd,. which had been set up in 1975 and which established Community Workshops in Enniscorthy and New Ross and a hostel in Enniscorthy, and which operated through a network of committees in practically every parish in County Wexford, were a continual source of inspiration and practical help. As well as this we had the invaluable assistance of the NRB who helped us to crystallise our ideas and develop concrete plans. All this came together in the concept of an Activity Centre for the Handicapped in Gorey.

The Activity Centre was envisaged for handicapped adults who are not capable of sustaining the level of activity appropriate to a workshop or open employment, but whose potential is such as to enable them to benefit physically, socially and physiologically from alternative activities. In general, all categories of handicapped were to be incorporated, i.e. physically disabled, mentally handicapped, some who have suffered from mental illness, and so on. The criterion for acceptance would be the ability to benefit and not the category of handicap.

This was one of the first such centres to be set up in the country and opened up exciting possibilities for the handicapped. It had been estimated nationally that four out of five of all handicapped adults not in an institution would benefit from such an Activity Centre. They were seen to need occupational outlets and an alternative way of life, access to gainful employment or a workshop situation, and their families required the aid and relief of not having to care for and occupy them round the clock.

The new building was on a one acre site and comprised work area, storage, some classrooms, general purpose room, bed-room, bathroom, kitchen, canteen, medical centre, office etc. Staff includes a Manager, Deputy Manager and part time cook.

The Centre originally took in eight trainees, in November 1981, when it was officially opened by President Hillery. At present there are twenty-eight trainees. The training covers social training, table behaviour, speech, hygiene, toilet use, bath, hair, cooking, setting table, washing up, remedial, numbers, shopping, phone, work, crafts, occupational activity, gardening, leisure, music, dancing, games, etc.

The approach and programme of the Centre has been flexible and adapted to the needs of each individual trainee. The interests and the needs and the level of development of each individual trainee is recognised in the individual programme created for each trainee. The majority of the trainees are full-time, attending five days each week. But some trainees only attend one day a week, others for a few afternoons and some only occasionally.

The local community is actively involved through regular functions and visits by parents and other groups. Over twenty volunteers help in the programme of the Centre for a few hours each week. An increasing number of individuals and groups informally visit the Centre or attend functions there. Particularly gratifying has been the wide and spontaneous financial support we have received from various local groups.

Naturally we have thought of the need handicapped people have for social and recreational opportunities. We sponsored a meeting of the eight local groups who work for or with the handicapped. Amazingly this was the first time these groups met to exchange views and experiences. They set up a regular monthly social evening for the handicapped attended by over eighty handicapped people and their families. Indeed the Centre itself is developing as a focus and facility for all handicapped in the area.

The local branches of the Irish Handicapped Children Pilgrimage Trust, the Association of the Arthritic, the National Council for the Blind, the Multiple Sclerosis Society and a number of other use the Centre's facilities for their meetings and functions, providing a whole new range of social and recreational activities for the handicapped. The trainees have been involved for the past eight years in the Special Olympics and this has proved an exciting and fulfilling experience for participants.

In November 1981 none of us would have foreseen the success, the progress and the happiness experienced by many of the trainees in the past twelve years. They are linked together in a happy, stimulating and pleasant atmosphere. The surroundings, the layout and furnishing of the Centre approximate to a home rather than a factory. At the moment, we are beginning a review and hoping to develop a plan for our development for the next decade. The more one does, the more one realises needs to be done.

In 1989 we established a small Pre-school service for children with mental handicap or development problems. Five children attended and it represents a great convenience and resource for the children and their parents. In 1990 we built and opened a Day Care Centre for the elderly attached to the Centre and at present we are making plans for an eight bed hostel for the elderly. A Social Club for the handicapped was set up at about the same time. We have also tried to develop a programme of spiritual care for the handicapped in terms of liturgies, prayer services, carol services, talks and so on.

I mention all this not to suggest that we are exceptional but rather that we are typical of many communities who try to make the integration of the handicapped a social and pastoral priority.

We have still a long distance to go before we have achieved an acceptable quality of life for all disabled people. Our experience has made us think deeply about the problems of the handicapped. Their biggest problem arises not so much from their handicap itself. They can come to terms with their limitations and can capitalise on their assets and abilities. Training can help them to develop to their full potential. Their problem is rather society's attitude to them. Does the community accept them? Does it realise their abilities and appreciate the contribution they are ready to make? Does it offer them the security and status which is their right? Or does it think primarily of their limitations, their defects, their disabilities?

They have less material attachment; they are more aware of God's presence, less complicated in their faith, less measuring in their love, simple and child-like in their ideas and hope. The handicapped are indeed what the old Irish phrase described as, 'Duine le Dia.'

c) *The Elderly*
The ultimate aim of all statutory and voluntary efforts with the elderly is not just the health or comfort of the old, but their happi-

ness. Old age is not an administrative problem. It is the challenge of helping a significant section of the community to experience joy, fulfilment and contentment. The greatest need in old age is undoubtedly happiness and the degree to which we can provide it for them can justifiably be used as a yardstick with which to assess the quality of our society. Like adolescents, old people are entering a new phase of human experience. They have the same elementary needs - security, independence and freedom of choice. It can be extremely difficult in another way, for many people over sixty-five. The sources of their satisfaction in many aspects of their lives are diminishing. A whole range of problems often seem to come overnight – loss of work and income, loss of health and sometimes home, loss of relatives or close friends. Each stage of life has its own peculiar qualities, its strains and hardships, its rewards and pleasures. Old age should bring the ultimate resolutions of all tensions, the satisfaction and tranquillity of a task completed, a job well done. It is not always so. Decline of physical strength can bring pain and enfeeblement. Impairment of mental faculties gives rise to humiliation and anxiety. Social isolation can come with the death of contemporaries and the movement of children and grandchildren to other areas.

Life, formerly so full and useful, can become empty and meaningless. It is here that the work of the caring agencies and the ongoing, loving concern of neighbours is important. Activities, services and facilities for old people,.such as the tremendous work of Old Folk's Clubs, can transform the lives of the elderly. They can help to make old age a haven of contented rest at the end of a useful and busy life.

One of the very positive things in recent years is the extent to which old people themselves are more actively involved in decision making in Clubs and Centres. For eight years now, we in the Gorey Social Services Council, have been running a weeklong programme of events for the elderly, each May, which is based on those ideals and principles.

However, I fear that our attitudes to the elderly are generally not as sensitive and supportive as they were twenty years ago. In particular, there is the problem of ageism. This basically means a discriminatory attitude to older people seen in this way: they are stereotyped in the media, sometimes as cantankerous or silly or useless or even sometimes wicked. Whenever individuals or groups are labelled by society they often begin to assimilate the assumptions behind the labels, whether these assumptions bear any resemblance to reality or not. So, if society at large adopts a negative view of older people, this can be assimilated by older people themselves. In a predominantly youth age, where the focus of thought and action is provided not by yesterday or by tomorrow, it is of crucial importance that we make positive efforts to help old people feel important, valued and with a real continuing contribution to make to their families, their neighbours and their society.

Services for the Elderly
Services for the elderly may seem in theory to be extensive. Often in practice they are not.

The care of the aged is a very good example of this. 1965 was designated 'Old People's Year' in this country and led to the establishment of a vast number of clubs, centres and services for the elderly. I feel that the time has now come to take a fresh look at the situation and the needs of the elderly in every area. There is an interesting parallel to this in Britain. In 1965 the Salvation Army produced a report which shocked public opinion in the United Kingdom. Roughly twenty years after the establishment of the Welfare State, the accepted view was that poverty had disappeared. Yet this report, called 'Tragedies of Affluence', discovered that there were approximately 400,000 children in want, 675,000 elderly people neglected and 700,000 social outcasts ignored. The structures for helping seemed to be there and in theory nobody was in want or neglected. There seems to me to be evidence in Ireland recently to suggest that the time has come for us, twenty five to thirty years after the great burst of social concern and provision of the sixties, to re-examine the extent and effectiveness of our services for the deprived. Public concern about individual social issues ebbs and flows – an ideal or a problem much talked about at one stage can be forgotten about before the ideal is implemented or the problem solved.

There are two further points worth mentioning. The most important thing for all of us is contact, communication and friendship. Every human being in every situation and at every part of his/her life needs it. Not very long ago at a Seminar we held on the elderly in the community, there was unanimous agreement that the most important single service to the elderly is regular visits by family members and by neighbours. It is something that many of us hear daily from the elderly themselves. Many old people in rural areas are extremely isolated and usually do not have access to the range of services that old people in a town have.

We have found that our Day Care Centre – where old people meet and enjoy themselves, have meals, talks and demonstrations and have access to chiropody, hair care, bathing, and laundry facilities – greatly increases communication and reduces the loneliness and isolation of many rural elderly.

d) The Unemployed
A well-known English writer once remarked rather cynically that the Good Samaritan would have been better occupied in organising a police force on the road from Jerusalem to Jerico than in spending his time on a single traveller who fell amongst robbers. Surely the Christian ideal is a society that does both. One major problem today that should be disturbing our consciences and steering us to immediate, concrete and widespread action is unemployment. It was rightly described by the bishops, in their recent pastoral 'Work is the Key', as the greatest single social problem facing the country. This problem is one to which the Churches have not really responded to any perceptible degree, yet the Churches are the one community agency that could make a substantial response to unemployment and all the spinoff problems associated with it. In a serious crisis, it is the Christian duty to pick up the wounded but also to work towards eliminating those situations and conditions that cause the crisis to happen.

Back in 1941, the great Archbishop of Canterbury, William Temple had this to say:

> The only real cure for unemployment is employment. In other words we are challenged to find a social order which provides employment steadily and generally, and our conscience should be restive till we succees. Christianity demands this.

These words are even more relevant today than when they were written. Real pastoral support, springing from deep Christian conviction, has wide dimensions. The Archbishop underlines that in attending to the immediate aspects of a problem and helping an individual which Christanity demands that we do, we must never lose sight of our ultimate ideals.

Unemployment for most people is a nightmare. We need radical changes in the re-distribution of wealth, the shortening of the working week and the reduction in the age of retirement, but economists say that this would spell economic disaster. Here is a challenge that Christians must face, because it is not going to leave us, and indeed may lead to serious civil unrest. Does all this not suggest that those who have jobs need to examine their consciences seriously about excessive demands for wage increases and so on? Are not such demands plainly immoral and unchristian in our present situation? Umemployment in Ireland is a festering sore. We must somehow learn to feel with the unemployed if we are to understand and take it seriously.

Loss of a job is similar to a bereavement. We are concerned and sympathetic when it occurs but in a short time the bereaved person is left to his/her own devices. But the fiercest backlash often comes months later. So too with unemployment/redundancy. It is not enough to be supportive when it occurs or sympathetic in a vague way. It requires long-term pastoral support and ongoing concrete help. We, in all the Churches, have done relatively little in this area. In my view, we need to devote time, thought and effort to working out responses and the nature of our services to the unemployed. Because many of us have never been without a job we find it hard to sense and feel the painful experience of unemployment.

Three of the most widespread results of unemployment are:

Boredom, with each day as the previous one and life lacking any landmarks or stimulation.

Loss of Self Respect, with all that means in terms of feeling less complete a person, doubting yourself, feeling not wanted. There is even a kind of psychological loneliness that goes with unemployment which all too easily corrodes all relationships with family and with friends.

Loss of Freedom, which lack of money causes. Shortage of money effects the basic choices of life – food, clothing, social life, holidays, toys for children, education.

Unemployment undermines our understanding of human work which Christian tradition has always seen as a major instrument of personal fulfilment and of community benefit. Particulary disturbing is the increasing number of young people who are unable to find any work from the moment they leave school and so many of them are growing up without the experience of work discipline which makes it harder for them to become mature or to cope when some new opportunity does arise.

As I have already said, the Christian response to social problems should be a combination of idealism and realism, a passionate commitment to the ideal, combined with sensitive acceptance of the real situation. The Christian couldn't be complacent either with a system that tolerates such appalling levels of unemployment or with the inadequate responses of society to it. Side by side with that, we should not disregard new training, occupational and employment schemes that are there. They may be short-term and inadequate in several ways, and manifestly incapable of stemming the tide of unemployment, but they do offer something. What in practical terms should we the local Churches be doing? Let me summarise what Julian Chorley, in his booklet 'Pastoral support for the Unemployed' recommends:

Challenge the system, lobby those with power (politicians), criticise injustices and highlight the problems.

> *Explore the possibility of local employment schemes.* Gather information, call people together, provide the back-up to get some local response.
>
> *Discuss unemployment with the heads of local schools,* on the basis that future employment situation must be top concern to educationalist.
>
> *Re-build community pride.* A good community spirit is a constructive context in which to help individuals.
>
> *Help change attitudes and provide understanding of the unemployed.* It is not only the unemployed in our Churches who need help. Those who are employed need to be helped to understand their Christian responsibilities.
>
> *Ensure a warm welcome and full integration into parish life for those who are unemployed.* Perhaps this is the greatest service of all we can offer. Unemployment creates isolation, with consequent depression. To be accepted as an ordinary human being with opportunities for activities and to serve other is a great reassurance.
>
> *Personal assistance of various sorts can be done on an individual basis.* Enabling people to act for themselves, helping to assess skills, counselling, providing regular responsibilities are among these.

We hear much today of the Church's preferential option for the poor. What I'm saying is that the pastoral care of the unemployed is a number one priority for the Church in Ireland today. The Church should provide hope, support, encouragement, concrete opportunities and practical help for the unemployed. The Church's preferential option in Ireland today should be for the unemployed.

e) The Carers

One of the new needs that has been recognised over the last decade is that of Carers.

I am convinced that responding to the needs of the carers will be one of the great challenges of the 1990's in the area of personal social services. Gorey Social Services Council has decided to make this a focus for thought and action. There is a general acceptance now that the best form of care for all but the most difficult cases of mental illness or disability is in the home. Few could deny that home care is caring care. Nor should anyone deny that it has only been the army of many thousands of ordinary citizens, most of them women, who have been prepared to sacrifice so much to look after elderly or ill relations at home, who have prevented the whole system from collapsing. This should be recognised by the state in terms of greater financial support for them, and an adequate carer's allowance paid directly to them. Progress in this regard in the budget three years ago is very welcome, but inadequate. It should be recognised by the community in terms of more voluntary support and leisure opportunities for the carers.

And it should also be recognised by other family members who don't allow all caring tasks to fall to just one member of the family. Indeed, I think that carers need some sort of Ad Hoc group which they would establish themselves and where they could exchange experiences and discuss difficulties.

Let me list some of the specific elements in an adequate and positive programme for carers:

A full range of back up service in the community (day care centres, transport, clubs etc.)
> A sitting service, to allow carers time for shopping and social life.
> Training for carers to discharge physical skills such as lifting, bathing a disabled person.
> The opportunity for carers to take a holiday.
> As I have said, an adequate carer's allowance.

Community Care policy, if it is to be successfully independent, needs to recognise and support the role of carers, otherwise we are only providing social welfare on the cheap.

When I talk of carers I mean someone who in his/her own home looks after:
- A handicapped family member.
- An elderly parent.
- A terminally ill person.
- A person who takes the place of a deceased parent.
- A person who looks after an elderly neighbour on a regular basis.
- A person who has to look after an elderly relative or parent for a short time who is recovering from hospitalisation or coping with a bereavement.

Of course carers sometimes get some personal satisfaction and fulfilment from caring. They have a very well developed sense of duty, and many are willing to undertake superhuman self-sacrifice. There are many many thousands of such carers who provide an unbelievable, dedicated and caring service day in, day out with little support. But they deserve better. It is truly shameful that there has been so little recognition of their needs or highlighting of the problems they face until the caring takes over their emotions and their social life. They should not have to care alone.

We set up a Support Group for Carers three years ago in Gorey. It meets monthly and has already established itself as a key factor in trying to improve the lot of local carers.

CHAPTER 11

The New Creation and the New Generation

In the mid 1960's almost every youth club or youth group had a clergyman either actively involved or associated in some way with the group. In the development of youth work generally in the 1960's the Churches had a very significant role. At that time many bishops had seen the value of having priests trained in youth work at various professional courses abroad. The development of youth services in their areas tended to centre around these men on their return and the level of development of youth services in these regions which have trained youth officers was measurably ahead of every other area. I sense today much less involvement by clergy in different aspects of youth service and the number of dioceses which have an adequate diocesan youth service could be counted on the fingers of one hand. I also feel that what involvement there is has progressively become narrow and restricted to more explicit religious programmes and services. As it is a time of ever growing disillusionment with, and alienation from, the Churches, this is an unfortunate development. Even against the background of extensive state provision for youth work in Britain, most dioceses have one full-time trained diocesan youth officer and a number have two.

In addition to that, a number of dioceses have an arrangement where one priest in each deanery has responsibility on a part-time basis for youth work. There is also an active and staffed (National) Catholic Youth Service Council. This is the sort of provision, in terms of trained personnel and wide-ranging pastoral programmes, which seems to me to be required in each diocese in the country for a number of reasons.

Firstly, the Church must serve the young. The needs of the young today are not only as great but greater than ever before. The fact of being young means they are in a particularly vulnerable and formative period of their lives. No one can be unmoved by the increasing number of young people who express their unhappiness with society by vandalism, violence, drug taking, or by withdrawing completely from the life of the community and trying to create a society of their own, based on their own values. The young go their own way, make their own rules and, in large numbers, disengage from society, not without reason.

Secondly, the Church should have a commitment to youth services because it wants to preach the gospel to young people and help them to grow to Christian maturity. The young within the family of the Church are often referred to as the Church of tomorrow, and so they are. But a positive attitude to them will only be present, when they are treated as part of the Church today. If they are not treated as part of the Church today, there may be no Church tomorrow.

Thirdly, the Church should see youth service as important because the youth service shares some common ideals with the Church, ideals such as personal development and growth, community building and social concern, social analysis and social change.

Youth and religion: difficulties

In my experience of working with young people and discussing religion with them, their difficulties tend to centre around three general areas. In the first place, there are those religious difficulties which derive from unresolved personal, moral or developmental problems. A difficulty associated with sexual development, for example, can create longterm problems if the young person does not experience sympathetic understanding and the opportunity for realistic discussion. A young person's difficulty with religion then can arise from faulty religious counselling/ spiritual direction. The long term result may be the apathetic practice of religion and, in some cases, the abandonment of it.

Secondly, I have known young people whose religious difficulties arise from an imperfect understanding of religion. It may be that they can't see the wood for the trees. They may have failed to get an overview of Christian beliefs and values which represent an attractive and convincing vision of life. Today's young people want an intensely personal faith and a religion of joy, one which speaks to them where they are in life and in the context of the kind of world in which they live and move, especially the one into which they are moving. Programmes such as Search for Christian Maturity and the Exercises in Christian Living have often provided such an experience for young people.

They may often fail to see the relevance of religion to life or think that it just does not make sense. This sort of difficulty results from a faulty religious education. I remember some years ago a very worthwhile discussion with a group of young people about the contents of Populorum Progressio, which clearly appealed to them. Their final comment was: 'But this courage, urgency, commitment does not correspond to our experiences of the Church in our parish.'

A third general type of difficulty young people have with religion is very much a contemporary one and is related to Church structures. This is the feeling that religion as practised and organised is useless, outdated, a definite hindrance to human progress and social development. For some sensitive and questioning young people, the apparent wealth/luxury of some Church personnel, the seemingly irrational public image of some ecclesiastical authorities, and the apparent preoccupation with financial matters and buildings become stumbling blocks.

How should we respond?
One of the most fascinating and inspiring parts of the New Testament is the Acts of the Apostles. There we see a simple, radical and attractive vision presented and embodied in a particular life style which gave the early Christians an extraordinary degree of courage as missionaries determined to pass on to others the life and teachings of Jesus Christ. It is there, among the early Christ-

ian Communities, that the contribution which religion can make to people's lives is seen at its best. There seems to me to be four basic elements involved:

Christianity Provides:

(a) A new experience which was and is the most basic and far-reaching a person can enter into – an experience of a personal relationship with God. (People do grow and develop on the basis of widening experiences and new personal relationships.) The early Christians' lives were changed utterly by this experience.

(b) A meaning to one's life: Religion helps to present a meaning in life – what is the purpose of human existence? how did the world originate and where is it going? These are the sort of questions that concern thoughtful young people and which all young people need to face. It is a commonplace of psychology that personality can disintegrate and character break down if one does not see any useful purpose to one's life. This meaning in life Christianity provides.

(c) A plan for Life: In the early Church, Christianity clearly presented a plan for life, a set of distinctive attitudes and values. Young people readily accept the need for a set of values, a system of behaviour. What concerns young people especially is how faith changes people, what it makes them do, what it achieves in day to day life. Sadly, very often they feel that religion has no relevance to life or think that it just does not make sense.

(d) Finally, the early Christians were part of a strong, supportive and sharing community. People, and especially the young, feel the need for community. All Christians need a community. If people are to lead a Christian life they need to be associated closely with others who share their spiritual outlook on life and who can support them in their pursuit of gospel ideals. The early Christian Community was that sort of community which lived out together and passed on to others the life and teachings of Jesus Christ. Most parishes today are not that sort of community, or at least don't seem to have the welcome, the courage and concern for each other that the early Christian Community had.

These four qualities of the early Church were strikingly evident in the Act of the Apostles but today in our Churches they are not nearly so evident. Many young people seek Christ and the deeper values of life, but not always within the Church. Indeed, many claim the Church has nothing to offer them as they search for meaning, for value, for community.

The evidence of the disillusionment with the Christian Churches among the young, and the dramatic fall off in youth interest in the Churches over the past two decades, has been well documented. More serious still, in my view, are the underlying uncertainties and scepticism about particular aspects of basic Christian beliefs and practices which are very clear even among those who are committed to the Church in terms of regular attendance and so on.

A major religious task today is to give hope, to help young people find a meaning in their lives and a set of values by which they can live, and to enable them to experience a warm supportive and sensitive local Christian Community. All this suggests the need for continuing reform and renewal at all levels of the Church and also the need for a wide-ranging pastoral programme to reach out to those who do not practice, to strengthen those whose faith is at risk and to help all young people to achieve Christian maturity.

Individuals and groups within the Church should face up to questions such as:

> What place is there for young people in the Church?
> What particular needs and problems are young people experiencing in the Church today?
> What responses should the Church make to these?
> What it the potential of young people?
> In what ways can the Church as a whole facilitate the development of this potential?
> In what ways should the Church help the development of flexible and wide ranging opportunities for them to make their contribution?

Let me finally refer to three major difficulties which need to be overcome:

1. Too many of us don't make sufficient effort to listen to and understand the feelings, the concerns, the expectations and the felt needs of young people. We don't, for example, appreciate how delicate, complex and agonising is the search for meaning and values that many young people are involved in.

A pre-packaged set of ideas and values, which are presented in a language of another age and which are proclaimed as self evident when, to the young, they are mystifying, are not likely to be either helpful or listened to. We need to enter the experiences, the thinking and the environment of young people. Otherwise we will never know or hear them as they really are. We will project our experiences and environment onto them and so end up speaking to ourselves.

The basic demands and needs of young people may be the same from one generation to the next, but social situations and environment do change. These changes create problems and difficulties and they have significant influence in shaping the thoughts and influencing the actions of young people. Their attitudes, concerns and priorities are significantly different from those of young people ten years ago. Their whole conceptual framework operates on different presuppositions and criteria. To be effective we need to come to know and understand the young person, his concern, his world and his experiences.

Many of us are unable to comprehend or appreciate how differently the young think and react today.

2. I think there is not yet a realisation in the Church of the serious pastoral problem that the dissatisfaction of the young with the Church represents in Ireland today. Many priests are concerned about their pastoral impact on young people. They may sense that in the view of a fairly significant number of young people they seem irrelevant.

Despite this, the pastoral care of young people does not appear to be given the priority it deserves. Our second response, therefore, is to treat the care of the young as a number one priority.

3. The third difficulty is the absence to date of a comprehensive planned response to this challenge. We have failed to plan a broadly based and comprehensive programme at all levels of the Church to respond to the challenge posed for the Church by the young. A major pastoral programme would include the active and planned encouragement of a whole range of spiritual, liturgical, social/community service and apostolic programmes for the young, available in all areas and open to all young people. A good deal of experimentation and many initiatives have taken place, but they have not yet become sufficiently widespread or integrated into the life of the Church to have the sort of impact that is necessary.

When we talk of specialised apostolate and pastoral programmes within the Church, we must strike a balance. We must avoid the danger of dividing the Church into generations and therefore of violating the unity of the Church. On the other hand, there is a specific call to care and minister to all groups of people. The existence of a very large young generation (50% under twenty-five – the youngest population in Europe) makes this sort of specialised programmes of pastoral care of young people an inescapable task.

Youth work within the Church, or outside it, is not a hobby. It is a serious business, a necessary consequence of the process of differentiation in which levels of our complex society need their own special attention. The greatest single challenge facing the Church is to help each new generation to become a new creation – mature, informed, committed and active Christians.

Irish young people and the future
The young today live in the worst of all possible worlds. Unemployment. violence, hopelessness are everywhere. A major task of Irish society today is to give hope to young people and a positive social role and enabling them to have warm, sensitive and constructive experiences and relationships.

Since the early mid 1980's there has been a dramatic deterioration in the employment prospects of young people. Youth unemployment rates rose sharply until the late 1980's. Associated with this is evidence that the brunt of the social and economic consequences of the unemployment crisis has been borne by young people from working class backgrounds. All this, in turn, showed itself in the unprecedented levels of youth emigration. In late 1987 I.M.S. published a survey/study entitled 'Young Ireland' for the Irish Youth Foundation. Its results added up to a fairly damning indictment of Irish society by the coming generation. Young people expressed a deep-seated concern about the general direction in which they saw Irish society heading and a real anxiety about the prospects the country holds out for their own future. The Report summarises:

'They are widely critical of the older generation in their conduct of the affairs of the nation. Their perception is exacerbated by the fact that very many young people feel marginalised in the political and economic life of the country. They sense that their potential to contribute in these areas is effectively stultified by those of the older generation who control the reins of power in the economic and political processes. Fear of unemployment is very widespread among young Irish adults and against this background it is hardly surprising that the prospect of emigration preoccupies a substantial number of young people.'

CHAPTER 12

Working with Young People

How I got involved in youth work
Up to the early 1960's youth came somewhere near the bottom of the list in society's concerns. It was a kind of Limbo – real life began when you emerged from it. Then in the early 1960's things changed with great speed. Youth was in the forefront of the world's concerns. Young people spoke to each other across national boundaries, they determined the agenda, they provided the vision, they set the pace. The 1960's was indeed a youth age. The young felt that they had inherited the earth. In every field of human endeavour, political, social, educational or religious, the framework of thought and action was provided not by the past but by the future and the future is always the territory of youth. It was a spectacular shift. To have been a student in the late 1960's was a tremendously stretching experience and one that I shall always greatly value.

In those days, one difficulty was that seminarians could not work during summer holidays. We were supposed to wear black. We were in fact supposed to act as 'mini-priests' with a very restricted role. For that reason, I was delighted at the opportunity provided by Fr Tony Scallan of Enniscorthy to go as a leader for three weeks each summer on a summer camp to Morriscastle, where we lived and worked with up to a hundred young people.

Fr Scallan himself had been the initiator of a very successful youth club, St Patrick's Boys Club, in Enniscorthy. I suppose this was my first involvement in youth work and I think from him I gained a sense of the importance of special provision for, and contact by the Church with, young people. Around the same time in my native parish of Bunclody, a young curate, Fr Aidan Jones, was pioneering a new style of mixed youth club, which was to be copied in many other areas.

After ordination I was back in Maynooth as a post-graduate. I was to help with the setting up of a youth club in Maynooth. This was a very useful experience for me and obviously I built on what I had learned on the camp and in Bunclody Youth club. It was the first opportunity that I had to be the overall leader of a youth club.

The function of youth work
Perhaps the most useful thing is to sketch the story of that fairly typical youth club – the needs of the local young people which brought the youth club into being; the function it saw itself fulfilling, and the way it went about achieving this end. The needs of the local young people, as I gradually came to see them, convinced me of the need for a youth centre and determined its characteristics. These could be summed up in three key words: association, education, social activities.

Association
In general terms, anyone working with young people comes to sense their questioning, their doubts and their uncertainties. Many adults just don't know what to make of young people. Probably the reason that the young person is something of a mystery to older people is that he is also something of a mystery to himself. He is trying to find himself, to establish himself as a person and this makes him unpredictable and, in ways, inconsistent. He is in a transition stage of development, a sort of no-man's-land between childhood and adulthood. He is not really accepted in adult society and no longer at home with children. The young person does not find the home to be the same haven of rest and comfort it was in earlier years. So young people need a place to meet and find security amongst themselves.

As well as this, I found that there was a deep-seated snobbery and class-distinction in the Maynooth area. The young people did not really know each other and did not meet regularly. This created the atmosphere in which prejudices and misunderstanding grew. So the club tried to be first and foremost a place where young people could meet, exchange views and enjoy themselves in a relaxed sort of way.

A small group of young people working together on a task, like preparing a debate or organising an old folk's party, can quickly come to know and appreciate each other. As they work and play together as equals, barriers are broken down gradually. Above all, the club must be their club not something imposed on them by adults. Ideally, apart from a few adult leaders, the club should be self-directing, in the sense that the discipline, organisation and management of the club should be in the hands of a committee elected from amongst and by the members. 'A boy gets to be a man when man is needed,' says John Steinbeck in *The Long Valley*, underlining the fact that young people become mature and responsible by being given genuine responsibility. A new committee was elected every six months. In this way it was hoped that the valuable experience of leadership and responsibility would be shared by as many as possible.

Education

I found that the young people of the area had nowhere to go in their free time and nothing worthwhile to do. So the club tried to provide worthwhile activities which would be of value educationally and recreationally. By taking part in the sometimes demanding club activities, young people gain self-confidence, experience of community life and of the attitudes and problems of others. Here they have the opportunity to make judgements, to form their attitudes and to inform themselves on relevant subjects. Young people nowadays are questioning and enquiring and this led to the emphasis our club placed on education – education, not in the narrow sense of books and lessons, but in the general attempt on the part of the members to better equip themselves to meet the challenges of life. Religion, politics, sex and marriage, drugs, gambling, social problems were just a few of the subjects the young people heard about and discussed. Recreational activities were provided too in ample proportions – rings, darts, singing, dancing, concerts, boxing, physical training and so on.

Social Activity

The local organisations, I found, could not be said to have the support of the young people. Probably the main reason for this was that the control of these was in the hands of a fairly small clique representative of only one 'class' or group in the area. Many of the young people were either disinterested in or critical of the local organisations, or found it impossible to play a part in them. It is a very unhealthy situation when young people are alienated from the main figures in the community and from those who are to the fore in local organisations. So it seemed necessary to create some sort of structure through which young people could contribute to their community. Young people are sometimes accused of being inward-looking and many youth clubs did tend to create teenage ghettos which hinder rather than help young people in becoming integrated in adult society.

Modern youth work must be directed towards integrating club members into adult society, by giving them adult responsibilities and activities, by providing contact with worthwhile adults and by giving them opportunities of contributing to their local communities in constructive ways.

So we had regular visitors to speak to and work with the members. We had youth club representatives on various local organisations, such as the Parish Council, the Old Folk's Committee, Muintir na Tíre, and so on. The youth club also, initiated various community activities itself – a schoolboys' summer camp, a children's party, a junior club, a number of charity walks, a concert in aid of two local charities and so on.

So the youth club was trying to provide an opportunity for young people of the area to form a group where they could meet in an atmosphere of friendship, equality and co-operation, where they could develop their characters and personalties and where they could make a contribution to their own community.

The senior branch of the youth club, with over eighty regular members, was open to young people of the area in the age range of 15 to 23. The junior branch, with a membership of over sixty, catered for the age group 12 to 15. Both groups met once a week.

The senior club met on Wednesday nights from 8.30 to 11.30 and devoted the first fifteen minutes to a business meeting conducted by the committee and at which all the members were present. It is, I think, important that a club should be conducted as an adult organisation and the members must be treated as young adults. At this meeting plans were discussed, duties were allotted and reports were received from various club officials. This was followed by an hour's educational activity – debate, discussion, lecture, film, demonstration, panel discussion and various activities based on then-popular television programmes, like Quicksilver, Twenty Questions, Know your Partner and so on. During the last hour and a half there was a record hop with opportunities for games like rings, darts, table tennis, etc.

Outside the main club meeting night, we tried to develop special interest groups. On one night a week about forty of the boys had boxing and other groups had music sessions, dramatics and so on. Soccer, basketball, handball and hockey leagues were also arranged. There are countless other small groups, within the club. In planning an imaginative programme, we tried to have, as well as these regular indoor and outdoor events, regular annual events – annual general meeting, club concert, club dance, club outing, one-day retreat, folk Mass, inter-club party, annual flag day, children's party and so on. The character of any young group is determined by the facilities for the needs of the young people in that area.

I hope that this detailed account of the life of one club might suggest the positive role a youth club can play in any community.

Youth Clubs United Together
I came back to Wexford in 1969 to teach in St Peter's College, and the Ferns Diocesan Youth Service was then developing. I got involved in it and that involvement, in turn, lead to my involve-

ment with the National Federation of Youth Clubs. From 1973 to 1974, I worked full time with the National Federation at a key time in its development. I shall always be grateful for the good fortune of working in the National Federation as General Secretary, for the opportunity to shape and influence a national organisation in a key time in its development for the people I met, for the events I took part in, for the experience I had, and for the warm camaraderie that was always associated with national Federation functions. I am also grateful, of course, for the broadening of ideas and the development of skills that resulted for me personally.

At that time, almost every town in the country was interested in setting up a Youth Club. These, for the first time, were mixed, and were also broadly based in their programmes because they were interested in not just keeping young people off the streets and out of trouble, but also, as I have said, in providing a wider range of social and educational activities and in trying to involve young people in various community programmes. The National Federation of Youth Clubs, the representative body for these youth clubs, naturally underwent some very substantial and far-reaching changes around the same time. I think that this resulted in a very strong and integrated vision of youth work.

There were four distinctive elements in this new thinking: Firstly, it was founded in an Ecumenical Christian Vision. Secondly, it believed strongly in a democratic and participatory approach to all decisions. Thirdly, it was committed to a de-centralised organisation based on regions and federal structure and, finally, it underscored the value of youth work and experiential learning in the context of social action.

At that period one of the things that I personally was very actively involved in was trying to raise the profile of the organisation, building a case for youth work and laying the basis for regional structures. This, in turn, especially with the media interest, led to government action on this front. In the mid 1960s there was virtually no statutory funding for youth work. The contribution and involvement of the Churches and individual clergy was a crucial factor. The annual grants for all aspects of youth work in 1969 was £100,000 compared with £9.8 million in 1991. I would estimate that full-time personnel involved in youth work in the mid sixties numbered no more than fifteen, while today the number is approximately five hundred. Few of us would have predicted the solidity and comprehensiveness of the youth services of today.

There has been a strong emphasis on professionalism of service, not just to meet common development needs of all young people, but to provide them with social education through different youth clubs, groups, special projects and also to meet the special needs of the disadvantaged young people who require additional degrees of support and help.

The sort of specialised services needed include information and advice centres, drop-in centres, coffee bars, youth encounter projects for early school leavers, neighbourhood and community youth projects, special programmes for young addicts, the homeless and disadvantaged young people.

During my period as General Secretary, I travelled to each of the regional groupings of Youth Clubs, and made a study of Youth Provisions in Northern Ireland. As a result of this, I prepared a report called 'Investment in Youth' which got fairly widespread publicity and I tried to spell out the implications for Youth Work and the developments that needed to happen in Federation Services.

I identified four pressing problems: inadequate club premises and/or the refusal of many school managers to make their facilities available; the need for more full-time trained regional officers; the lack of training of voluntary leaders, the limited range of club services and the need for more extensive work for different age groups and for new regional areas.

I tried to use the report to carry out a double campaign which was fought out over the next few years. Through newspaper and television coverage, and in many religious and social journals, the public was educated about the need for a national youth policy and substantial investment in youth work. For almost two years, from 1974 to 1975, the Federation was in the forefront, fighting for recognition of the education value of youth work and for both Church and State to take it seriously.

President Childers backed the youth cause and began to appear at many Federation events around the country, completely changing the public image of the Presidency.

Press coverage of the N.F.Y.C was magnificent and the annual Gormanstown conference was captured with pages of text and photographs in the morning dailies, an event of social significance in its own right.

On another level the report was used to lobby John Bruton, who became Parliamentary Secretary to the Minister of Education in October 1973 in the new Coalition Government. He was the first minister of State to take youth work seriously and the instigator of a wide-ranging study in his Department. He eventually did prepare a youth policy.

One of the other areas I particularly enjoyed and benefited from were the international contacts and exchanges which became a source of inspiration, broadening the horizons for key persons in the Federation. The first formal contacts were made with the European section of M.I.J.A.R.C.. Relations with European groups quickened in 1972 when Derek Nally became involved with the European Youth Foundation. In fact, at that stage we established our own international committee. People attended major world and European Youth Conferences and gatherings of all sorts. Derek Nally was one of the people who made a huge impact in Europe.

In 1974, the British, the Danes and ourselves set up the European Confederation of Youth Clubs, which has now become a major funding source and co-ordinating body on a European level. I was privileged to sign the Protocol of Accession at the founding Conference in 1975 in Denmark and I served on the Executive Committee of European Confederation for two years. There is no doubt in my mind that the sort of forward-looking liberal approach of the Federation was greatly strengthened by these European Contacts.

There continues, of course, to be gaps in provision, and serious concern about the level and timing of Government funding. Despite this, the whole range of youth services and programmes is now generally felt to be necessary. Trained youth personnel are now accepted as having distinct professional skills and perceptions. The youth service has helped many young people find their way better, personally and socially. Without the youth service over the last twenty-five years, many young people would be less free, less articulate, less concerned, less aware and less mature.

The youth service is something unique in the educational system. Unique in the first place because it develops totally different techniques and relationships between leader and member, from any other level of education, unique because its range of activities, and unique because it competes with virtually every other form of commercial and social activity.

My involvement in youth work today is very limited. One of the more recent areas that I found personally very enriching has been in the establishment of the Irish Youth Foundation, which is basically a fund-raising and grant-giving agency predominately made up of business people. This was established in 1985 and since then in excess of £2,000,000 has been raised or pledged and in the region of £1,000,000 has been disbursed to all sorts of youth projects. This money supplements state funding and also grant aids projects for which state funding would not be forthcoming. In my view, it has made a significant impression in the overall youth services in the country.

CHAPTER 13

Communicate or Die

A wartime head of religious broadcasting at the BBC said, 'The Church must communicate or die.' We could make it our motto! Fr Martin Tierney, in his excellent book, *The Media*, puts it in these words:

> The Church is the community of those who believe in Christ as God's communicator ... the Church is called to live out the unlimited communication of God's love, reconciliation and wholeness to the world ... communication is at the very heart of what the Church is, calling people out of estrangement into communion. There is no Church without communication.

Engagement with the Media
'Go into the world,' said the Risen Lord, 'and preach the gospel to every creature.' With these words he launched his followers into two thousand years of engagement with the Media and wrestling with Media issues.

Down through the centuries, Christian communicators have wrestled with these issues and have sometimes come up with tremendously effective answers. There is no doubt, for instance, that the impact of Reformation ideas was greatly helped by Martin Luther's understanding and maximum use of the recently invented printing press. The pioneers of missionary radio made a bridgehead for the gospel in many countries and cultures where traditional missionary methods would be either unwelcome or ineffective. One could multiply examples from other centuries of the

Church being in the fore in utilising new communications opportunities.

By comparison, we fall far short of their efforts and achievements. The Media have, in many ways, replaced the pulpit as the most important source of information, ideas and attitudes. The Church would do well to recognise the Media as valuable new pulpits provided by our age. If we do not, we are retreating from the market place and ignoring the crowds to whom, in the words of Pope Paul VI, we are called to 'Preach the gospel from the rooftops of the world.'

Christians link into the media in five ways:

a) We are receivers

All of us are concerned with the media as consumers or receivers. We have the opportunity as individuals and in groups to make our view known as to what we want or don't want coming into our homes. We have a duty to try to see that standards are maintained. We also have the choice about what to watch, read or listen to. We bemoan the fact that television has killed conversation or limited neighbourly visits or family communication. If that is true then the remedy is within our own power. We limit our dependence and create alternatives. We also need to be much more critical and discriminating of what values and attitudes are offered to us. We need to be aware of the effects that the media may have on us and we must judge what is being communicated and, if necessary, refute it. While there has been occasional talk for the last twenty-five years on the need for media education, virtually nothing has been done in our school system to provide it.

b) We are participators

By this I mean that we offer a service to those who work in the media in providing regular information, facilitating media personnel who may come to cover Church events, occasionally taking part in television Masses and services and so on. As far as I know, only a few dioceses have a Press Officer who is active. How many religious orders have a PR officer? Do local parishes or units of religious orders have some one responsible for generating positive and regular media coverage? What level of resources, personnel and finance is available to the few who have such an office? Church media offices are of central importance to the Churches' mission in today's world.

I am very fortunate, as Press Officer for the Diocese of Ferns, to have a generous publications budget, a Fax machine and generally a situation where my opinion is sought. For all I know, I may be in a minority of one in the country.

c) We are performers

There are vast opportunities for the Church in this area but also a great reluctance by Christians, lay and clerical, to appear on radio and television to express and explain and defend their religious viewpoints and values. Something quite radical needs to be done about training in communications in our seminaries and houses of training, and there needs to be comparable training opportunities for Christian lay people which would help them in articulating gospel values.

d) We are transmitters

We have priests who provide columns for local and national papers and we have a large, strong religious press in Ireland. Three Religious weeklies circulate here. The Irish Catholic (37,000), the Catholic Standard (3,500 approximately) and the Universe (7,000 approximately.)

One of the great new opportunities of our lifetime is the arrival of local community radio and the independent television channels which are imminent. Local Churches have played their part together with other local community groups in establishing and maintaining local radio. There is also great scope for small production units in the local Churches who would prepare programmes on religious events, persons and topics which could be made available to local radio stations.

The recognition of this new opportunity led the four Church leaders in the Diocese of Ferns and county Wexford to establish an

Inter-Church committee in 1988 with the aim of developing a blueprint and strategy for the Churches' involvement in local radio. This in turn led to the establishment of the Christian Media Trust, a company representative of the Churches to oversee their interest, to link into South East Radio and to develop a range of specific services.

In brief, Christian Media Trust acquired a 25% shareholding in South East Radio with two seats on the Board and two places on its Programmes Advisory Panel. A purpose-built studio at St Peter's College, Wexford, allows us to produce programmes to the highest possible standards as well as being a valuable training facility which is increasingly being used by individuals and groups.

We were invited to produce four hours of religious programmes each week. Our aim has been to provide a varied, attractive and lively package and one that is distinctly Christian. The feedback is very positive and suggests to us an appreciative and growing listenership. The Training Sub-committee has offered a range of training opportunities of different types tailored to suit the needs of different groups. The recently established Information Days for schools have proved popular and The Diploma in Radio Skills, organised by the Adult and Community Education Department in Maynooth, was an intensive and professional course offered for the first time outside the College.

The Evaluation Group has begun its work more recently and in the future will grow in importance as a vehicle for audience participation, which will guarantee that our programmes are relevant, effective and comprehensive in scope.

The role of C.M.T. has been important as the most intensive form of day to day co-operation between the Churches. In many ways it is unique: the highest shareholding and involvement in the management of any local radio station in the country; by far the largest number of hours of Religious programming in any station; one of the few and the most up-to-date studios owned by the

Churches in any area; and the widest range of other activities and services.

On of the things that continues to amaze me is that all of this could have been done without the services of any full-time staff person. It has been a totally voluntary organisation demanding a huge commitment of time, effort and talent from a small core of highly dedicated people.

Two overall worries should be noted. Will it be possible to continue and extend our wide range of involvements into the future on a totally voluntary basis? We are continually looking for new ideas, approaches and volunteers. The second big concern relates to finance. But for the fact that there was an unplanned and unforeseen overrun in the initial capital costs of the studio, we would be in a comfortable profit situation on existing budget figures. We have tried to maximise the use of the studio commercially and we have also done some fundraising recently.

The success of local radio generally has been quite amazing, even though it has had to operate on playing fields that are far from level. Virtually all the stations in the country had substantial accumulated losses resulting from higher than expected start-up costs and losses in the early years of operation. The cost of transmission facilities and buying into a news service have been substantial.

Local radio stations pay a levy of 3% of gross revenue to the Independent Radio and Television Commission. This, it seems to me, is quite inequitable. No other industry is required to pay the operating cost of its regulatory body in this way. The recent removal of the cap mechanism on RTÉ's advertising revenue, while desirable in itself, should not have been done in isolation. As it is, it allows RTÉ to reduce its advertising rates and maintain income at the same level. It has allowed RTÉ an unfair advantage over the local radio stations.

To level the playing field and allow the local stations to clear off accumulated losses and develop the quality of programming, a number of steps should be taken by the minister:

(a) A certain percentage of the licence fee (perhaps 10%) should be set aside for the development of local radio stations.

(b) The IRTC, which has had a key and very positive role in the development of local radio to date, should be further refined and extended.

(c) Specifically, the IRTC should be given control of local transmission facilities; it should set up and operate a central news service which would provide national and international news to the local stations; it should take a developmental role and provide training courses and programming development initiatives for local radio.

In the face of all the inequalities and disadvantages, local radio stations have made striking progress in terms of gaining listenership. Taken together, they have now surpassed the listenership of Radio 1 and have almost twice the daily listenership of 2FM. They have become truly local in responding to the tastes and reflecting the concerns and distinctive features of local community life in each area. They have also progressively increased the level of access and involvement by the local communities. In the process, they have reinforced local identity, community pride and, indeed, democracy. They deserve urgent help to overcome the sort of difficulties mentioned above and, more important, to maximise their real potential for further significant development.

Let me finish with a quote from Bishop Comiskey: 'Future generations will not be kind in their judgement of us if we fail to seize this great new opportunity in a spirit of deep Christian courage and faith.'

e) We also are Providers of an 'alternative' service
A priest's expertise in using the technology of the mass media is never a substitute for the pulpit, the friendly conversation in passing, the home visitation, involvement in local community projects. One of the success stories by the Churches in communication in the last decade has been the rapidly growing number, and generally high standard, of Parish Newsletters.

There is another important sense in which we provide an alternative service. Much more serious than the alleged unfair treatment of the Church is the underlying view of what constitutes 'the good life' which sections of the media accept and put across. A basic task for the Church is to present attractively an alternative vision and lifestyle which is truly Christian. At the end of the day, every Christian is the message as well as the messenger, as is very strikingly expressed in the following piece from Australia entitled simply 'You':

> You are a walking advertisement of your Church and the Christ whom it proclaims. You take the Church out of its four walls, and make it live in the everyday affairs of life. In fact, what people think of your Church, they think of you.
>
> The preaching in the pulpit is fruitless unless it is reflected in the lives of members of the congregation. Christian teaching is ineffective unless it comes to life in the attitudes and behaviour of people. Your Church is measured not so much by what its leaders say as by what you do.
>
> It is easy to make speeches and claims, but claims must be validated by the product. You are the means by which the good life advocated by the Church is communicated to people. Your Church professes a concern for people; you express that concern in the way you act towards others. Your Church tries to build up a Christian world; you validate these attempts by your conduct on the job or in your community. Your Church claims to have a gospel that will make people new, opening to them a more satisfying life; you are the demonstration of that claim.
>
> Your daily acts as Christians preach more sermons, teach more people, and save more lives than the words that are spoken inside the four walls of your Church building. Without you, the Church has no life.

A Media Age

Television, radio and newspapers are so much part of our daily lives that we tend both to over- and underestimate their importance. We can overestimate the effect that the content or approach of an individual programme or even a specific series has on people's behaviour. At the same time, we underestimate the changes brought about by the presence of the mass media in our society. They are part of the twentieth century landscape and, like all landscapes, they have grown familiar. Engagement with the media is an urgent matter. No Christian can opt out. The media are not in business to make better Christians. If we don't work out how the media should fit into our lives, they may well make us worse ones.

Media Inadequacies

There is no doubt that some coverage of major issues inflames, trivialises or distorts. Undoubtedly the Bishop Casey affair was one of the biggest Church stories this century. As press officer for the Diocese of Ferns during that period, I was dealing with a lot of media queries, both Irish and foreign. Indeed for one week it was running into about twelve to fifteen a day. This was so for two reasons: Firstly, Bishop Comiskey had acted as a 'go between' for Bishop Casey with the Papal Nuncio and, secondly, and quite coincidentally, there were three priests from the Diocese of Ferns who had sought leave of absence at that time. I felt that RTÉ, the Irish Times and the local Media in Wexford treated the two issues in a fair and balanced way. Some sections of the Irish Media weren't fair or balanced. The Irish Independent chose to make the departure of the three priests their lead story and linked it to coverage of the Bishop Casey affair. I felt that these three fine young men were seeking leave of absence to reflect on their ministry and future lives and that they wanted space and time and privacy to reflect. Instead of this their names were blazed across the front page of a major newspaper. The mother of one of the priests was unfairly and excessively pressurised to give an interview, which she refused to do. As well as that, the decision to take leave of absence is not a sudden one. It is clearly something they would have been considering and consulting people about for a long time.

There was one stage during that period also when there seemed to be open season on all clergy. The amount of gossip, rumours, and innuendo was staggering. This situation was only defused when Bishop Comiskey decided to meet it directly. In doing this he did a signal service to clergy who were being unfairly and maliciously treated. This was a sad episode in some sections of the Irish Media.

Lessons for the Church

As I have said, there are faults in the press, and I am sure journalists would be the first to admit that there is always room for improvement of standards and correction of weaknesses. But we Church communicators must accept some responsibility for some of the unfairness in coverage. When press comment appears critical or dismissive of Church concerns, it may have an important lesson. It may serve as a mirror in which we can see ourselves and our efforts to communicate. We can realise that what strikes the onlooker about our efforts is sectarian, bickering, or preoccupation with trivia.

I have never heard any public Church acknowledgement of the fact that the Irish based national papers have generally avoided the sensationalism, the gross inaccuracy and sheer stupidity of the British tabloids. More specifically, there has been very little appreciation of the efforts by the papers here to avoid what John Horgan has called a 'casual, careless or indifferent approach by the newspapers to the public they serve'. These efforts include things like a corrections and clarifications sections, various right-of-reply devices, and the appointment of readers' representatives. The latter may be only a first step but should we not acknowledge it as, in John Horgan's words, 'a small but significant milestone in Irish Print Media history'?

We don't really appreciate that those who work in the Media have an extremely difficult task. They have to keep their readers without compromising standards. They have to balance the public's right to information against the individual's right to privacy. They have to withstand pressure from organised interests and from approaching deadlines. They have to balance various artistic and technical considerations. In my view, the Irish Media are getting these balances fairly right most of the time and providing a more positive service than they often get credit for.

The Church ill-adapted

The Church has never sufficiently adapted to an information age and new communications technology. It often seems to me that the Church has never fully acknowledged some basic social developments of this century, like freedom of speech, freedom of conscience, freedom of the press, and an egalitarian and participative society.

The Church has a preoccupation with secrecy. If the media are not assisted or given adequate information, can we complain if what they write appears trivial, incomplete or out of context? Again and again over the years, I have heard from friends of mine in the media that the one major agency which is most unaware of the importance of good presentation of news, and least willing to give information, is the Church. As Gerard Priestland asks, 'How can we publish material if those who know it won't tell it?'

Too many Church people are afraid of the media – afraid not only of 'going public' but also of the technology of radio and television. I have always been amazed that clergy who, by their very vocation within the Church, are in the business of communication, receive little or no training in media ministry. Indeed a common reaction in the Church to clergy who frequently receive media publicity is to see them as lovers of the limelight and seekers after publicity.

Media and journalistic training needs to have a much higher priority in policies relating to personnel and pastoral life in the Churches. Effectively preaching the gospel means years of theological study – study of the message. Surely there should also be the same period devoted to becoming skilled in the Media. For every thousand who professionally study theology, are there more than a handful who professionally study the Media? How many who have talent for the Media are encouraged and facilitated in using it? In fact it has been agreed that there are fewer priests professionally trained and involved on a full-time basis in communications than there were twenty years ago.

CHAPTER 14

The Religious Press

The Church by definition is a community. A community must have some way of perceiving itself as a community, of conversing with itself to formulate its experiences and judgements. For many Christians the instrument of this perception and conversation is the religious press.

The number of religious magazines, journals and papers here, as against our total population, is one of the highest in the Christian world. The quality is improving and the variety is great. Every dimension of Christian living and thinking is provided for: catechetics, the priestly life, the religious life, the foreign missions, youth, the pastoral fields of practice and preaching, the special magazines of movements like the Pioneers, Charismatic Renewal, the Vincent de Paul Society, the contemplative life, specialised theological and pastoral journals, religious newspapers and some high-quality religious magazines for general readership.

The News Function
Public affairs which involve religious issues and values are appropriate subject matter for the religious press. To live mature responsible Christian lives, people must have the information needed to be aware, and the opportunity to decide how they should respond and to recognise what contribution they can make. Specifically, the religious press provides information about authoritative statements, about national and local programmes, about developments in worship, ministry and education, and about key Church personnel and major Church efforts. It also offers to society a means of seeing how events are perceived and valued within the Christian community.

The Forum Function
The religious press provides a facility where people can reflect on the Christian message and seek its fuller application in complex, changing situations. It should reflect the wide range of opinion and judgement which is found in the Christian Churches. It debates and analyses, and it tests various opinions for their consistency with Christian teaching and values. It communicates to Church authorities the shifts of opinion and the shoots of new life that are going on among the people of God. In the words of Paul VI, the religious press can be 'The antennae of the Church'.

Implicit in this is the same obligation that all sections of the media are bound by – to tell the truth. Old apologetic attitudes die hard and can lead to the suppression of inconvenient or discreditable truth. An editor can be caught between his duty to edify and his duty to inform. *Communio et Progressio*, talking about the secular Press said, 'It is right that freedom of communication and the right to be informed be established in law and guarded from excessive pressures that might weaken them.' It is an equally important principle that the religious press should be free from such pressures itself.

The Educational Function
There is, too, the educational function of the religious press. Books, journals and magazines provide a wide range of educational services to the Christian community, from aids for teaching right through to presentation of the most sophisticated theological thought. It is probably the only effective channel for the distribution of important documentation and information on liturgy, music, religious education, social services and so on.

The Religious Press Association Survey
The Religious Press Association, an Inter-Church Agency with forty-three publications, was established in the mid-1960's to improve the quality and develop the influence of the religious press in Ireland. In conjunction with Irish Marketing Surveys, we sponsored a survey in May 1991 of the readership of the religious press and the following summary of its major finds may be of interest.

Background

Three-quarters (75%) of Irish adults see their religious beliefs as important in their lives. Almost one-quarter of adults (24%) admit that religious belief is of limited or of negligible importance to them.

Women generally attach far greater significance to religious beliefs than men do. While almost one-third of adult men (32%) attach little or no importance to religious beliefs, the same is true of only 15% of women. Markedly greater significance is attached to religion by older people.

The importance attached to religious beliefs is broadly paralleled in patterns of religious observance. Three-quarters (76%) of adults identify themselves as at least weekly Church-goers. Again, regular observance is markedly more common among women than among men, among older people than among the young, among the farming community than among other social groups, and in rural areas generally compared with urban areas.

Readership

Readership of religious publications in Ireland continues at a fairly high level. Over four out of ten adults (42%) identify themselves as readers of one or more religious periodicals. One quarter (25%) of the adult population identify themselves as 'regular' readers of one or more publications. The residual portion would be 'occasional' readers.

The general readership profile for religious publications is substantially biased towards women. Two-thirds of the total number of readers are female (although women only make up one-half of the national population). Adults aged 50 years or over are also considerably more significant (41%) in the general readership profile for religious publication than the proportion they form in the population as a whole (32%). The farming community and rural dwellers generally make up a disproportionate element of the readership profile for religious publications.

Broadly speaking, these anomalies in the patterns of readership of religious publications, by comparison with the structure of the adult population as a whole, are reflected to a greater or lesser extent in the profiles for individual publications.

Nearly four out of ten (36%) readers of religious publications subscribe to one or more periodicals. In global terms, the same proportion (36%) acquire the publication through either a local school or the local Church. Between 10% and 20% of readers purchase copies from a promoter. Other outlets such as newsagents and bookshops are of relatively limited importance.

However, quite substantial proportions of readers of religious publications, averaging around 15% across the range of publications, do not in fact buy the copies they read. They acquire them from other readers.

The articles of most interest to readers of religious publications are those relating to missionary activities, those dealing with social and moral issues, and features dealing with family life. Articles concerned with hobbies or Church developments are of widespread but of somewhat less intense interest.

Non-readers

One-half (50%) of those who do not read religious publications give lack of interest as their main reason. The only other serious reason advanced by a significant proportion of non-readers (16%) is that religious publications are not available. While there may in some cases be a need for rationalisation, the finding does indicate the importance of widespread distribution and display in winning over the less-committed.

Marketing

In a Christian society there should be a major market for religious publications. Unfortunately our marketing techniques are too uneven, haphazard and too restricted to Church-related settings. We have too few sales outlets in the mainstream of life and business. Religious publishers need to be more forceful in the secular market. In the UK (which would possibly be considered a post-Christian society) the major secular publications and bookshop chains find that there is quite a significant market for religious books. They reckon that this is an area easily targeted and one very responsive to promotion. There is clearly a need in Ireland for closer collaboration among publishers, retailers, advertising personnel and specialist outlets to give more prominence to religious publications, to expand awareness and availability of religious publications and to help to increase sales.

Challenges facing the Christian Communicator
1. The challenge to evangelise effectively
Effective communication of the gospel in a clear, comprehensive, coherent and attractive way is the key challenge for the religious communicator. In many ways we have been hesitant and introverted, almost afraid to preach the whole gospel message and vision. I think, for example, that most modern people are not obsessed by sin, continuously afraid of death, overwhelmed by injustice or racked by disease, but they are desperate for meaning – for a vision, for values, for explanation, for God. The preaching of the gospel today must respond to that particular felt need.

Talking about liturgy, which should be a clear communication to all who are present, Gerard Priestland says, 'An enquirer who went to Church today hoping to find out what Christianity was about would probably be mystified. He or she would witness a ceremony for the initiated - not a reaching out to the hungry'. Are our religious magazines for example focused more on the initiated than reaching out to the hungry and the searching? Are our magazines still too churchy and ecclesiastical, with a high concentration on new jargon and valid but limited and incomplete insights? How many of them would be suitable for placing in the hands of anyone who is not already deeply committed to the Church? How many of them would truly help intelligent enquirers about Christianity or those agonising with the basic questions of meaning?

2. The challenge to respond to the needs of the young
One of the great concerns of the Church should be to communicate the gospel effectively to each successive generation of young people and help them towards greater commitment and Christian

maturity. Would *Hot Press* encourage a column such as Fr Brian Darcy's in the *Sunday World*? An effective Christian column in *Hot Press* would reach an audience that might rarely have a Christian message directly addressed to them in an immediate, open and intellectually challenging way. Such an exercise would be worth committing to two or three full-time personnel.

We rarely think of effectively preaching in the real market place. We need to be brutally honest in assessing how directly and successfully we are communicating the gospel, from the many pulpits available today, to all sections of our population and society. Our religious publications should seriously ask what youth-focus do they have and in what ways are they responding attractively and convincingly to the culture, the perceptions, the voiced concerns and felt needs of the young people.

Surely publications such as these should be of some help to young people in developing an awareness of God, exploring aspects of Christian theology and attempting to live according to Christian morality. We should also try honestly to face two key questions: Why, increasingly, do the Churches fail to keep children as they grow up in their teens? Why do we not attract more young people? When I say face these questions, I mean try to analyse, in a professional way, why this loss, this failure to attract.

3. The challenge of questioning 'New Paganism'

Large sections of the media have accepted, without adequate analysis or questioning, the new economic and social directions in Irish society in recent years. They have failed to raise the real problems that have resulted from the often uncaring attitudes and the narrow values that are driving these changes.

4. The challenge posed by fundamentalism

Fundamentalism is a very strong and growing feature of the contemporary religious landscape. Fundamentalism often seems to have little to do with religion. It is more a state of mind: intolerant, exclusivist, full of covert hatred and bitterness, anti-intellectual and tribalist.

Many of us would agree with Archbishop Runcie's words, 'Religion has to have a certain craggy toughness about it, but it is my belief that faith should have non-exclusive confidence in itself. It is possible to be a fundamental Christian without needing fearful denunciations and words writing off other people and their faith.'

It was never more important to promote tolerance and dialogue and to emphasise common sense, individual choice and the power of human reason. In the context of recent advances in communications technology and opportunities, which have been truly staggering and are transforming our world, it is worth recalling that in America, in particular, new communication opportunities were utilised much more effectively by fundamentalist groups than by mainstream Churches.

They have drawn the biggest and sometimes rather nasty congregations plus the biggest telethon-type funds. That danger is something we must watch and the deeper question needs to be faced: How do we find a way to make a gentler, reflective, caring religion more effective and communicable in an information age?

5. The challenge to market more successfully

In this information age, the Word of God can easily get swamped. We need to make the Irish public more aware of the extent, variety and professionalism of the religious press, increase the number of people who buy them and, more importantly, those who read and discuss them.

The Religious Press Association's well attended and publicised Religious Press Awards were a deliberate first step down that road, and the monthly news release to the media generally on the contents of that month's religious publications, should facilitate the same process.

6. The challenge of working more closely together

The richness and diversity in the religious press in Ireland is a positive feature that needs to be encouraged and supported. Equally there needs to be greater co-operation, joint approaches to common problems and greater sharing of resources and expertise.

The Religious Press Association is the ideal location for this common action. We have begun to explore common problems and to try to do together some things we cannot attempt individually. When I was Chairman of the RPA, we held a Seminar on 'The Religious Press: Trends, Problems and Possibilities.' This was the first attempt to analyse and respond together to the range of problems and opportunities that we all face.

Conclusion
The religious press has a crucial role in sharing knowledge, experiences and concerns, but also in moving the frontiers forward and continuously helping to push out to many new goals, seeking new growth points, highlighting shifts of opinion, and isolating weaknesses of approach and understanding.

Pope Paul VI once said that journalists in the Church had a double function: to communicate downwards and upwards. The editor of a top religious publication has a key role. His appointment is at least as important to the future of the Church as the appointment of a bishop. He reaches people on a regular basis and he probably communicates more effectively than many pastoral letters. By editing a major publication he has considerable influence in shaping attitudes, projecting issues and challenging to action and development. Some years ago a very shrewd Irish bishop said to me that the one person who most influenced the shape and promote the renewal of the Irish Church was J.G. McGarry, the late editor of *The Furrow*.

CHAPTER 15

Counter Witness

Many of us, who were students and involved in student affairs in the sixties and in youth organisations later, talked much about a New Ireland and worked for the ideal of a tolerant, open, concerned, forward-looking, egalitarian and peaceful society. Martin Cowley, in the *Irish Times* (August 13 1988), summed up our hopes: 'We used the terms as a new start, a revitalisation of shared national spirit, a new shared vision, and a combination of all the traditions in harmony.'

We do have a new Ireland today but the reality is in some ways a nightmare. It is a narrow, self-interested, violent, unequal, divided and, in many ways, an uncaring society. This is the context in which Inter Church Relations operate also.

Some wise person has said that 'the opposite of love is not hatred but indifference'. If that is true, it may help to explain why the Christian Churches are still separate.

Many of us remember when Roman Catholics and Protestants in Ireland had minimal or surface contact and were strangers to each other. Some of it no doubt remains. The price of this strangeness, even strife at times, is a Western World now described as post-Christian. The famous parable of the Vineyard gives us the clue. When Christians do not actively pursue the work of the Lord together, when they concentrate on what divides rather than what we have in common, then decay and destruction sets in. What unites us is infinitely more important and extensive. That lesson is gradually being learned but we have some distance to go, to become conscious of the full implications of this central truth.

We have not in particular taken on board the basic message that unity and reconciliation are at the centre of the Christian task. Disunity seems to have us under a spell – even when we recognise what is wrong with our world we seem to be able to do nothing to get out of this circle of strife, Yet, as Christians we believe that the spell is broken by Jesus Christ; He comes as the one who reconciles where there is strife. He forgave the sin that is always present in disunity and strife. He comes to unite us with one another and with God. He calls us to look at life and the world in a new way. He provides a new vision to develop peace, harmony, tolerance and understanding, forgiveness and love. Unity is what he willed and prayed for. Unity, promotion of peace and reconciliation, is a key service the Church provides to the world. Unity and peace is a central aspect of the Church's witness to the sovereignty of God. The scandal of the division among Christians is enormous.

Christianity, far from being the bringer of peace, becomes the bearer of strife and division and the gospel appears all the less credible as its claims for unity and love appear contradicted by the fact of disunity and religious strife among Christians.

The estrangement between Christians is most intensely felt in Northern Ireland. A first step is to end the violence. The vast majority of Irish people are opposed to violence and deeply wish for peace. But there are a number of factors which prevent this overwhelming desire from immediate universal and tangible effect.

1. In the first place, peace-making in Ireland has to cope with our history. Sir Horace Plunkett said that Irish History was 'for English men to remember and Irishmen to forget.' That is probably putting it too strongly, but our past is killing our future. Too often folk memories, not moral judgements, determine attitudes. Do we need to control our history and geography books so that they put forward values of peace rather than those of war?

2. Another impeding factor is a certain widespread failure to think through our commitment to peace. There is an ambivalence in our attitudes arising from political perceptions, from history,

from prejudices and so on. To be Christian is to be Pro-life. There can be no common ground with those who take or diminish life. An important Pro-life Movement in Ireland today is found among those promoting reconciliation and understanding and laying the ground work for peace, and the real anti-life movement is found among the promoters of hostility and division and those who openly or tacitly go part of the way with them.

Every subversive newspaper bought, every penny contributed, every prejudice repeated, every distorted reference made to history, every refusal to understand and see things from another point of view, every failure to support the Gardaí, every opportunity missed to speak out against or disagree with the supporters of violence, are in greater or lesser degree opportunities for peace-making lost, and many are allowing an environment vaguely supportive of violence to continue.

3. To be a Christian in Ireland today, above all else, in my view, demands that people do not yield an inch or travel a foot with the men of violence but move positively in the other direction, in the direction of understanding, co-operation, reconciliation and peace. One of the saddest things is that there is no concrete and constructive structure at which the abhorrence of the vast majority of the Irish people for violence and division can be forcefully and publicly voiced and be productive. A broadly based, but neither politically nor religiously based, peace movement in this country is long overdue.

We need to develop a peace mentality, programmes of education for peace, and a movement on structure through which Irish people can work on a constructive and ongoing basis for peace. Even when violence ceases, there will be the massive task of reconciliation to be undertaken. All of us must be humbled by those courageous Christians who are reconcilers. People like the families of sectarian assassination victims who can forgive their assassins and implore their own communities not to seek revenge, those who create projects of cross-community co-operation and understanding: these are the giants of practical ecumenism.

One should acknowledge that there have been real advances in Inter-Church relations in our lifetime. From the standpoint of the 1950's we have made spectacular advances. Let me illustrate it with the example of a dear friend of mine, the late Archdeacon William Parker who was rector of Gorey for almost forty years. When he came to Gorey first, contact with the Roman Catholic clergy was minimal. Attendance at each others congregations was restricted, if not discouraged. Yet at his funeral service the Roman Catholic Bishop was present and recited some of the prayers. There have been other advances, and particularly in the Diocese of Ferns, in the whole area of Inter Church marriages, in regular joint services, social integration, Inter Church Projects and so on. All this is solid and positive and, as I've said, from the perspective of the 1950's, progress had been spectacular, From the perspective of the 1990's we have still a long way to go.

Where do we go from here? The following might be ways to re-launch the Ecumenical Endeavour:

1. St Paul says that reconciliation between people is possible when they have been reconciled to God through the cross. Jews and Gentiles are reconciled when both are 'one in Christ'. As we come nearer to Christ we come nearer to one another. The more we are renewed in the image of Christ, the closer we come to each other. And, of course, there is the other side of this coin – if we do not draw closer to each, other we estrange ourselves from God also.

2. Inter Church relations need to be more strongly promoted as a key priority by the leaders of our Churches. We need prophets of ecumenism, like those of the 1960's, who will provide the vision and promote the courage to take new bold steps together and at every level of the Church.

3. We need very specifically to make the achievement of peace in Northern Ireland an overriding concern of all the Churches.

4. It is, of course, notorious that divided communities have different stories of the history which they share and which divides them. We need ways of developing a common history which

overcomes the distorted histories and the resultant bitterness, sense of grievance and even hatred.

5. We need more knowledge of each other's Churches, habits of devotion, exercise of authority, underlying basic religious assumptions and so on. These are obvious methods of advance in this area.

6. Theology and spirituality should increasingly be seen as a common enterprise. Why not joint clergy retreats? We should take advice and directions from each other's spiritual guides and read each other's spiritual books.

7. In liturgy and worship too there is room for further progress. Joint blessing and clergy involvement together in baptism and marriage are welcome, but here too more can be done. Why, for example, on a day like Good Friday can we not have a united service? There must be other occasions too during the year when we can worship together.

8. In education, our primary schools could work more closely together. In Gorey for the Unity Octave, the sixth classes of Roman Catholic and Church of Ireland schools meet for an afternoon at one of the schools, and later in the year there is a return visit to the other school. Again, there is infinite scope for development of this sort of contact and work together.

These are just a few obvious suggestions as to how gradually, but urgently, Christians could come closer together in Ireland.